In this delightful introduction to confessions of faith, Nathan Eshelman tells the story of the faithful God and his faithful people who have taken their stand on his Word. Eshelman shows that confessions are not mere arguments about words, but they are acts of worship and witness. In many ways, the future of the church depends on its faithfulness to biblical confessions of faith. Highly recommended!

—Dr. Joel R. Beeke, president, Puritan Reformed Theological Seminary

Some Christians only look back to the "good old days" and get stuck in the past. Others only look forward to "progress" and end up floating around without anchor or mooring. Eshelman models the biblical way of looking back at our historic confessions of faith in order to move forward confidently and safely. In doing so, he blends conservative truth with contemporary application, a much needed gift in our day.

—David Murray, senior pastor of First Byron Christian Reformed Church, author of Jesus on Every Page

I Have a Confession makes the case, with a focus on the *Westminster Confession*, for the important role confessions of faith have. Written for a broad audience, it will be particularly helpful for those unfamiliar with or with doubts about the necessity and value of confessions for the life and mission of the church in the world.

—Richard B. Gaffin, Jr., professor of biblical and systematic theology, Emeritus, Westminster Theological Seminary

Many learned commentators have already spilled gallons of ink on the history and theology of the Westminster Standards. Yet this new work by Dr. Eshelman is in fact a unique approach to this vitally important topic.... To say that it is popularly and clearly written is an understatement. The text engages the reader as it is sprinkled with interesting insights from Dr. Eshelman's own life and family experiences. . . . This is a highly recommended book that will benefit anyone new to the Reformed and Presbyterian tradition.

—Richard Gamble, professor of systematic theology, Reformed Presbyterian Theological Seminary

Biblical confessions of faith can help cure doctrinal laziness, evasiveness, and indifference. The extent to which that cure isn't wanted today is exactly why it is so needed. . . . If you are involved in a church that seems soft on doctrine and easily influenced by the latest theological fad or cultural movement, you should read this book. If you are a Presbyterian but aren't sure why, you should read this book. If you want to learn from competent guides how to experience God and live according to his revealed design you should read this book.

—William Boekestein, co-author of the illustrated children's book, *Contending for the Faith: The Story of the Westminster Assembly.*

Too many believers wander around the Christian landscape unclear of what the churches that they attend actually believe. Eshelman guides you to consider the importance of a church having—and holding fast to!—a clearly stated confession of faith. With a shepherd's heart and readable style, Eshelman uses scriptural warrant and understandable church history to lead God's people into an appreciation of the green pastures of the *Westminster Confession* with their well-placed, ancient boundary stones.

—Barry York, president and professor of pastoral theology and homiletics, Reformed Presbyterian Theological Seminary

Eshelman's *I Have a Confession* was a treat from start to finish. Espalier apple trees and carp fishing with a spear will help the reader to think better of a confession's role in the church's life and the authority of the Scripture in writing confessions. *I Have a Confession* is first aid for a church in trauma and a guide for her to develop spiritual muscles. . . . This is a book that will serve Christ's church.

—Jeffrey A. Stivason, professor of New Testament studies, Reformed Presbyterian Theological Seminary

I HAVE A CONFESSION

I HAVE A CONFESSION

The What and Why of the Westminster Confession of Faith

Nathan Eshelman

GRASSMARKET PRESS
PITTSBURGH, PENNSYLVANIA

Grassmarket Press

an imprint of
Crown & Covenant Publications
7408 Penn Avenue
Pittsburgh, PA 15208
crownandcovenant.com

ISBN: 978-1-943017-55-3
eBook: 978-1-943017-56-0
Library of Congress Control Number: 2022943829

Printed in the United States of America

Theological editors of Grassmarket Press: Daniel Howe and Kyle Borg.

Text font is Minion Pro set in 11/15 point. Chapter titles are Mr Eaves XL Mod Nar OT. Interior and cover design by Esther Howe. Photograph of Grassmarket Square is from the Reformed Presbyterian Church of Scotland. Used by permission.

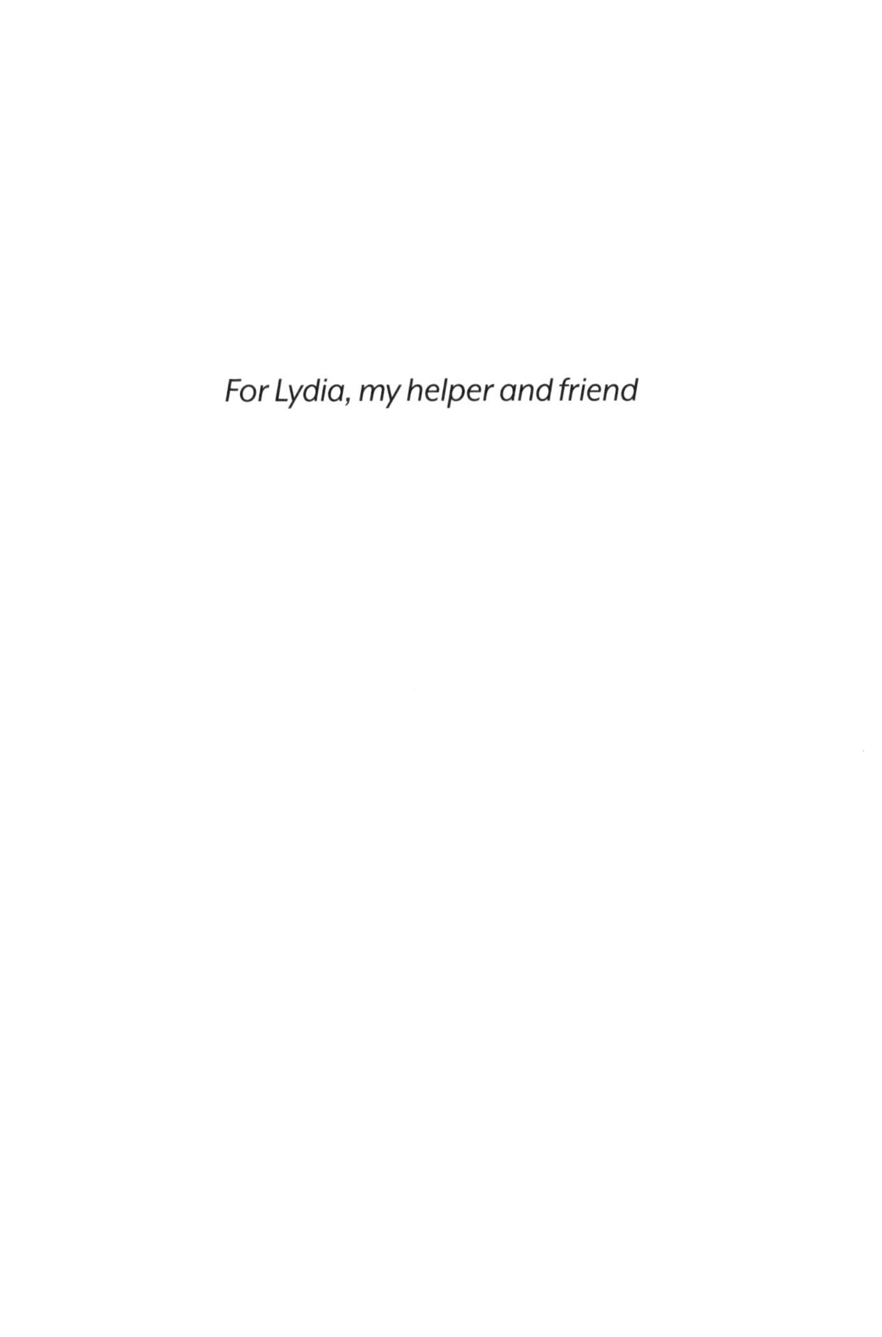

For Lydia, my helper and friend

CONTENTS

1
A POVERTY OF CONFESSING CHURCHES

THE EGGS AND COFFEE were overpriced, but the company was good. Paul and I met up at a neighborhood coffee shop right off The 2 highway in my former Los Angeles neighborhood. We had not seen each other in a couple of years although we had kept up through social media, texting, and the occasional phone call. As a college student, he left eastern Ohio and made his way out to the palm trees and never-ending sunshine of Los Angeles. He attended the congregation where I pastored for twelve years and always showed a bright future for church leadership, and still does. He completed a degree at a well-known Christian college and upon graduation made his way back to the Rust Belt of eastern Ohio. Over the last several years he has sold vehicles, formerly high-end German cars and currently heavy equipment. I was surprised when he ordered quiche—I guess you can take the man out of LA, but you can't take the LA out of the man.

"How's church going, Paul? What are the encouragements you've had lately? What have you been reading?" Paul and I quickly jumped into several theological conversations and much of the fellowship was sweet. As I cupped my hands around my oversized mug, I listened to his struggle in finding a church home that reflected some of the values and principles he learned and how he worshiped while living in Los Angeles. The conversation meandered around the "dead guys" (theologians) he's reading, the highs and lows of work, the young ladies who have come and gone, and funny, endearing memories of his time in Los Angeles. Throughout both the serious and lighter moments of our conversation, we kept coming back to one central theme: he desired to worship at a church that was rooted in historic Christian teaching, but one that also looked ahead to the future. Paul leaned in, his infectious smile turning sober, and said, "Pastor Nathan, I just want a church that I know will teach the same thing today as it will when my future children are old."

"You are looking for a confessional church, Paul," I said, looking him in the eye. "Exactly," he replied soberly.

In that moment of reflection, Paul expressed one of the great values of being in a confessional church—a church that has a solid, biblical written standard of belief. A confessional church believes and teaches a summary of the Christian faith that is written down for all to study. What does the church believe and teach about Jesus? What does the church believe and teach about the Bible? What does the church believe and teach about salvation? Confessions help us to summarize all of these questions (and more) that the Christian faith poses. My friend Paul understands the value of these summaries; he understands the value of being a confessional Christian in a confessional church. For me and the congregation that I serve, that confession is the *Westminster Confession of Faith.*

ESPAL-WHAT?

Have you ever gone on vacation and attended the local generic community church? Maybe you checked out their website and saw something to this effect:

"We teach the Bible."

"No creed but Christ."

Maybe the website featured words like evangelical or Bible-believing, or it mentioned that the pastor attended a seminary that you've heard of, but following the worship service, you couldn't shake the thought that something was wrong. Maybe you were unable to pin-point exactly what was wrong with the service or the sermon but had the sense that it did not reflect true biblical teaching.

Protestant churches have developed differently since the time called the Protestant Reformation. We could talk about Lutheranism, Anglicanism, or Presbyterianism—lots of isms—and they all look a bit different. However, churches that have a confessional statement that they actually believe and teach look like their confessional documents. Lutherans have the *Augsburg Confession*; Anglicans and historic Methodists have the *Thirty-Nine Articles*; Reformed, whether Dutch or German Reformed, have the *Three Forms of Unity*; and Presbyterians have the *Westminster Confession* and *Catechisms*. Each of the Bible-believing varieties of these confessional churches have grown up and around their confessional documents. Their worship and practices take the form of the confession that they profess.

When I first visited my friends Daniel and Esther at their home in Providence, Rhode Island, I asked for a tour. I've always been a fan of old houses—old everything, really—and I wanted to see their old Greek Revival home in the heart of the city. During the tour, Esther commented to me that there was an *espalier* apple tree against the garage to best utilize the space. *Espalier* is a French method of growing a tree flat against a trellis. The word means "something to lean against," and *espalier* trees literally grow flat, within inches of a building.

In many ways, confessional churches are like *espalier* trees. First, note that Bible-believing Protestant churches that grow with "something to lean against" tend to reflect their intended shape.

Bible-believing Lutheran churches look like the *Augsburg Confession*. Bible-believing Reformed churches look like the *Three Forms of Unity*. Bible-believing Anglicans look like the *Thirty-Nine Articles*. And those of us in the Presbyterian tradition, those that are Bible-believing, look like the Westminster Standards.

Without the confessional heritage giving churches something to lean on, much of modern evangelicalism and Protestantism has come to grow in ways that neither Protestants nor evangelicals ever intended. When the "something to lean on" was taken away, churches gradually stopped looking either Protestant or evangelical.

Much of what my friend Paul is looking for is a church that will grow into the same form it was intended to grow into. Without a standard—a written, biblically sound standard against which a church checks its beliefs and practices—there is no telling what sort of misshapen growth will occur. Confessions keep us from misshapen growth.

What is wrong with today's church climate is that the historic "something to lean on" has been broken down, kicked aside, or removed altogether. Psalm 80 talks about a vine that grew into a garden and then lost the "something to lean on." The psalm says:

Why have you torn down its fences? It is plucked by
each passing hand,
Forest boars have gnawed upon it, And wild creatures have pastured there.
Turn again, O God of Armies, Look from heav'n,
visit this Your vine.
So uphold what Your right hand did plant, And the
son You raised up in strength.

(*The Book of Psalms for Worship*, 80)

In many ways, I believe this is what we are seeing around us today as we look at the scarcity of hearty, doctrinally sound churches—the vine is there, and these may really be people who love God, love his Word, love Jesus Christ, and want to serve him out of that love—but they are unruly and wild; they are in need of pruning and taming. They need something to lean on. And since there is no *espalier*, the church grows unruly and without direction. We see this lacking too often in the church today. Many Protestant and evangelical churches have been left in a place of poverty as the safety and structure of confessions have fallen out of favor for a variety of reasons. The teaching is often poor, the worship is poor, and the commitment to God's Word is poor. And for those who are in this state of poverty, whether churches or individuals, the counsel here may be counterintuitive: rebuild the trellis. Have something to lean on. Those in a state of poverty rarely rebuild the trellis first, but that is what is needed in today's evangelical and Protestant climate.

I grew up in an old western Pennsylvania town at a time when the steel-related plants and factories were shutting down. Families that at one time could support a quality lifestyle on a one-income factory job were no longer able to do so. Many fell into poverty as jobs went away. When poverty strikes a community, things that were once taken for granted disappear. Houses don't get that refreshing coat of paint. Repairs that need to happen get set aside. As budgets get tighter and poverty's struggle becomes the reality for families, it shows.

In the midst of poverty, no one is going to attempt to solve a community-wide poverty crisis by working on the garden first or rebuilding the trellis as a way to fight the poverty. But in the case of the church (or individual Christian) that lacks spiritual focus or precision and yet loves God's Word, loves God, and loves the Lord Jesus Christ, the counsel I give is simple: begin growing around "something solid to lean on." Begin to see the value in the heritage of the *Westminster Confession of Faith,* and use it how it was intended to be used: to give direction to your spiritual life, or what you believe and how you live out what you believe.

Many will warn you that regaining vibrant "confessionalism," or using a confession, is not the answer that you are looking for. Many will tell you that not only is confessionalism not the answer, it is altogether going in the wrong direction. Why would a theological paper written in the 17th century have any value to your spiritual life today? I will answer that question in due time, but first we need to look at some of the reasons people may tell you that use of a confession, specifically the particular brand of it in the *Westminster Confession of Faith,* is not the answer. Let's explore some of those objections now.

BUT WHAT ABOUT . . . ?

It sounds strange to tell those in poverty that fixing trellises will increase their family income. It also sounds strange to say that reviving a connection to a 17th century document will benefit your current spiritual life, your family's spiritual life, and your church life. When Presbyterians hear objections to holding to the *Westminster Confession of Faith*, there should be some level of empathy toward those making the objection. Who is going to believe that fixing trellises fixes bank accounts?

Let's look at six reasons some may resist reviving confessionalism as a means to spiritual growth.

The Frozen Chosen

I spent my college and seminary years in Grand Rapids, Michigan. Grand Rapids is a center for Reformed denominations, colleges, seminaries, and bookstores.

Many Christians who were, let's say, less than excited about Reformed Christianity would sometimes refer to Reformed and Presbyterian believers as "the frozen chosen." The idea is that people who hold on to a confessional Christianity are unable to change, unable to discern the Spirit, and unable to grow in understanding of the Word. The accusation is made that some are stuck in their theological ways—ways that are hundreds of years old.

Having standards that are not intended to change or standards that are difficult to change (confessions can be revised after all) does not quench the Spirit or keep the church from having a full reliance on the Word of God.

At times, holding to standards like these is called "dead orthodoxy." Orthodoxy means right teaching, and to imply that right teaching can be dead is a compelling argument, but only on the surface. This can only be true when what we believe is separated from how we live out the Christian faith. What one believes should always influence and affect how one's life is lived out. The only way that orthodoxy can be dead, leading to a frozen-chosen mentality, is when belief no longer produces a love for the Bible, a love for God, or a love for Christ's church. Spiritual deadness in organizations that claim to be Reformed or Presbyterian cannot be traced to having a written, biblical statement of belief, but rather to not believing or teaching that written statement.

True, vibrant Presbyterianism believes, teaches, and lives out the *Westminster Confession*. This summary of what the Bible teaches on certain topics ought never lead to a frozen-chosen or dead-orthodox mentality, but instead it will invigorate the heart and help its followers grow in the knowledge of the Bible and the one about whom the Bible is written—Jesus Christ.

Google Seminary

We live in a time some call the age of anti-expertise; examples are all around us. Recently I was visiting my cardiologist for a checkup. As a minister, I need to stay on top of my health since much of my life is sedentary, spent reading books or seated with people for meetings or counsel, often over lunch. While waiting for the cardiologist in my drafty gown and feeling sticky from the recently removed EKG pads, I was reading the various posters and medication ads on his office wall. One read, "Google is not a doctor and Google search is not a diagnosis." For many, there is a tendency to trust Google over one's own physician. This stuck out to me as a perfect example of one of the reasons people may reject confessionalism—they distrust professionalism.

The medical field is not the only victim of this mentality. A bartender from the Bronx is seen as a better choice for New York's 14th Congressional District because she is not a career politician. The same can be said for the increase in reality TV over scripted television (as if reality TV is real and not scripted).

The church has not been exempted from this anti-professionalism. There are many graduates of Google Seminary that are quite happy being social media theologians and sermon critics after a quick Google search. This mistrust of professionals has led to a rejection of much of what has been done through the hard and prayerful labor of those who study and practice theology for a living. The *Westminster Confession* is a document that was produced by pastors, elders, and theologians through much debate and with many years of academic and linguistic training in the writers' collective background. For some, that is reason enough to avoid connecting oneself to Presbyterianism or the *Westminster Confession*. Many believe that a "me and Jesus" mentality (with a dash of Google) produces a more genuine and hearty spirituality. This is a reflection of the spirit of the age, not a reflection of biblical Christianity.

Washing Plastic Forks?

Once I had an open house at my home and about 100 people were invited. Due to the nature of the open house, we knew that others would invite people too, so we really did not know how many would come. Fifty plastic forks were purchased for the event as well as a hundred or so paper plates. Throughout the day and into the evening, people came and went enjoying a spread of meats and side dishes. Several times throughout the day, I walked around, collected the used plastic forks, washed them, and put them back on the table with the other plates and utensils. Occasionally I would get a strange glance while standing at the sink or the occasional comment such as, "That's extreme recycling there!"

We live in a society where everything is disposable. We are the paper plate and plastic fork generation. My grandfather would tell me that they don't make cars like they used to, meaning that today's were not meant to last. Of course they are not meant to last! No one wants to drive around in a 1973 Olds Cutlass in moss gold (that was a real color choice for the Cutlass) when the new cars get better gas mileage and have Bluetooth technology and touch screen this-and-that. As a society, we don't want the old and tried and true; we want new and fresh—we want to toss out or recycle in exchange for the newest and latest. Last year, I replaced my hot water heater and my plumber told me that they are not meant to be repaired; they are meant to be replaced. Like it or not, this is our culture. And in many ways, many of these things truly are obsolete.

The church suffers with this mentality as well. God's Word is eternal and applies just as much today as it did when it was written. As Christians, we know that. But those of us who claim to hold to and believe in a statement of faith that is nearly half a millennium old need to understand that our culture's mentality of obsoleteness slips into matters of faith. In the thinking of many, church needs to be fresh, current, and trendy. Old documents are none of those things.

If you've been in the Christian faith for more than a decade, you can reflect on some of the trends that were designed to increase your spirituality, commitment to Christ, or love for God. It may have been a bracelet intended to evoke ethical meditations, or a book that everyone was reading to learn how to have real purpose, or a swap-out of what's on the Top 40 radio station for the latest Christian music knock-off. The evangelical church wants what is new, fresh, and trendy, and many are willing to throw away last month's pop-spirituality for today's.

Confessionalism does not work well when one is chasing the latest fad. Using a confession works well when one realizes that the old paths—tried and true—are to be valued over the latest trends. Although we live in a plastic fork culture, we need to keep that mentality away from our church and personal belief systems. We instead need to realize that new is not always better—especially when talking about eternal truths. Yes, life has changed and the issues we deal with are different. Nevertheless, scriptural understanding that helps us navigate through today's dilemmas is as relevant as when the writers of the *Confessions* wrestled through what the Bible teaches on matters of life and faith.

Math Class is Tough

In 1992, there was a controversy over a talking toy. Outrage is not new to the 21st century. Teen Talk Barbie® was a toy doll that was equipped with a voice box that had several pre-programmed phrases. One of the phrases was "Math class is tough!" The National Council of Teachers of Mathematics protested the Barbie and claimed that the phrase was "detrimental to the effort to encourage girls to study math and science" (*The Education Digest,* 58, Dec.1992, 72–75). Whether Barbie could possibly discourage girls from entering STEM careers I will leave to the professionals, but let's be clear about something—math class is hard. Most people have to work at math and science in order to have a functional knowledge of the subjects. This should not embarrass any teachers' council since all things worth learning are worth struggling through. Concepts and technical language are part of math and science and will take work for anyone that desires to learn them.

A "math class is tough" mentality applied to confessionalism is a reminder that when we talk about the church's system of doctrine, we are working in the realm of science. Theology—the study of God—is a science. What do I mean? Questions are asked and answered, observations are made, and conclusions are drawn. And as this scientific method is applied to the Bible, a technical language or jargon develops.

When I was a kid, I had a favorite drinking glass that had CB radio jargon written on it. Phrases like "green stamp road," "picture taker," "Willy Weaver," and "ten-four" all fascinated me because it was a world that I was not familiar with. My uncle drove big rig trucks and knew all the jargon, but it was not used in my home because my father and mother were not in that industry. Jargon or technical language is used in all disciplines and all fields, and the field of theology is not exempt from that. Terms like "justification," "sanctification," "covenant of works," "sacraments," and others are technical terms that may take time to get to know, but the effort will prove to be worth it as one grows in grace and knowledge. Theology class is tough. I am okay with that.

Not everyone is okay with that, though. We hear things like, "I just want Jesus," or "just give me the Bible," and those may seem like legitimate arguments against using a biblical confession, but the thinking is shallow. You would not tell your daughter to take calculus and not encourage her to become familiar with the technical jargon that makes it easier for her. So, too, with Christianity. Over the past 2,000 years, a language or jargon has developed that helps the Christian understand what the Bible teaches about various topics, and it is worth the effort to learn the jargon of the Christian faith. Chapters 5 and 6 of this book will help in this area.

But the Bible?

We believe in the Bible, and the Bible directs our faith and practice—right? You may have heard the phrase "*sola Scriptura*" before. The Latin phrase means "Scripture alone" and tells Protestants and evangelicals that the Bible is the source and final authority in life when it comes to faith and practice. Well-meaning and honest Christians who love the Bible, love God, and love his church struggle with how we can hold to a Bible-alone position while also having a confession of faith. Do we believe the Bible *and* the *Westminster Confession*? Does the *Westminster Confession* make the Scriptures of less value to us? Some will turn to the words of the Lord Jesus in Mark 7:8 when he said that some disregarded the commands of God so they could keep the traditions of men. Is the *Westminster Confession* a tradition of men?

We need to be sensitive to this argument and at least understand where our brothers and sisters making this claim are coming from—however unfounded it may be. The *Westminster Confession* has literally thousands of proof texts that demonstrate how closely to the Scriptures the writers clung. A study of the *Westminster Confession* with your Bible open will prove that the Bible is the source for its information. Chapter 3 will explore more deeply why the church is able to write confessions and how those confessions do not contradict the idea that the Bible alone is our source of knowledge concerning God. Confessionalism based on a solid study of Scripture is not against the Bible or its authority.

Do What Works

The sixth argument against having written standards is related to the fact that we live in an age of pragmatics. If it works, go for it. We hear that all the time. And what works for today's society is bigger, faster, and more. Vancouver is one of my favorite cities in North America. There's something peaceful about it to me—big bridges, the sound leading out into the Pacific, tall pine trees and tall apartments, and that old-world-meets-modern feel that is so different from life in Orlando or Los Angeles. I am always taken aback when I am in Canada and an 8 ounce—or 236 milliliter—drink comes with a meal. It is just not "America big." America wants everything bigger, faster, and more, more, more.

In church life, the local megachurch is the place where people see Jesus working. "Of course he is working there—there's 1,000 or more people," one might reflect. But peer through the doors of the little Bible-believing Presbyterian church with seventy-five members and something seems wrong—something's not working. Where are all the people? If using a confession works, then why are faithful Presbyterian churches often less than 100 people when the McMegachurch down the street is serving thousands and thousands? Our American ears tell us that something is not working because it is not big and fast and more. Yet the Bible does not set the standard of faithfulness in terms of excitement, largeness, or speed. The false idea that confessionalism is wrong because it does not produce super-sized churches is to be rejected. Spirituality is judged in terms of depth, not breadth. Just because something seems to work does not mean that it is actually working. A wrench can hammer in a nail, but ought it to?

BACK TO THE FANCY FRENCH TRELLIS

After exploring these six common objections to using a confession, we must ask ourselves what we are to do. We understand dead orthodoxy, the anti-professional age in which we live, our throw-away culture, the lack of understanding and technical nature of the confessions, the so-called high view of the Bible, and the do-what-works mentality of churches, but what should the Christian do who loves the Bible, loves the God of the Bible, and loves the church? What should you do if you are seeking a deeper knowledge and experience of the Christian life for yourself, your family, and your congregation? I would direct you back to the trellis—to the *espalier*.

Confessionalism is both a safeguard and a guide for the Christian life. For the Reformed or Presbyterian believer, the *Westminster Confession of Faith* will prove, with effort (remember math class is tough), to promote a vibrant Christian life and experience. There are four ways that a return to the strong foundation of confessionalism will revive you, your family, and your congregation out of the life-draining poverty of the current state of evangelical Christianity.

Prompt Right Thinking

The Westminster Standards will prove to help check your thinking about certain theological topics against the teaching of the Scriptures. What do you believe about the Bible? What do you believe about God's character? What do you believe about the person and work of Christ? What do you believe about the nature of salvation? All of these questions, and many more, will come up in the life of the Christian, in his or her family, or in the life of a congregation. Our confession prompts us to begin thinking in biblical terms and categories when we think about Christianity. This is of great value. It has often been said that good fences make good neighbors. The idea is that fences keep neighbors out—but fences also keep us from wandering where we do not belong. Confessions are helpful to fence in our thoughts.

Promote Unity

One of the greatest discouragements for me as a Christian is when a church turns out to be much different than advertised. The problem with current confessionalism is that you cannot always tell what you are going to get—this is where the *Westminster Confession* comes in. Ministers who are unified around the confession encourage, challenge, and sharpen one another around those truths they hold in common. This unity around the term *Presbyterian* or *confessional Presbyterian* is a unity that is of great value. It is a unity of trust. The psalmist tells us that when brothers dwell together in unity it is precious. For all who want to claim the name Reformed or Presbyterian, their unity must be around what the churches have agreed to concerning theological truth. You are not preaching and teaching in isolation as a Presbyterian. If you teach something that is in opposition to Scripture, as understood in the *Westminster Confession*, you are accountable to the pastors and elders around you.

Protect From Error

No one wants to believe lies. As a kid, I was deeply offended when I learned that Santa Claus was a fairy tale. I am sure that I was overly offended, but even as a kid, I was sensitive to the fact that believing error was not a good place to be for a person. How much truer when truth and error are related to eternal things—eternal truths. The *Westminster Confession*, as it is built on the foundation of the Scriptures and 2,000 years of Christian theological reflection, is only promoting those truths that are considered essential in the

Christian life. And in that essential teaching, the *Confession* protects minsters and church leaders, as well as members, from falling into or promoting error. As a minister, I am under a vow to teach in accordance with the *Westminster Confession of Faith*, and if there is an area where I disagree, that is to be discussed with the other pastors and elders in my presbytery (a regional body of congregations).

Without a standard of written belief, anyone can say sincerely, "I am only teaching what I found in the Bible." Most, if not all, cults and sects will say that their particular brand of religion is merely teaching the Bible or recovering the true meaning of the Bible. Without a standard that says, "We believe A about this topic," then how can one be held accountable for teaching B if they claim that they found it in the Bible? We are all protected when we have standards that are both a solid, biblical safeguard and a guide. The *Confession* provides those outward protections from error that you and I need.

Proclaim What We Believe

The fourth way that the *Westminster Confession* is a safeguard and guide for us is that it makes us honest. My dad always said that he didn't care how much money a man had as long as he "got it honest." In the realm of church life and theology, the *Westminster Confession* keeps us honest. It makes a public proclamation of what we believe for the whole world to look upon, investigate, discuss, argue about, and hopefully come to embrace.

There are no fees to come and see what we believe; there are no monthly dues for going deeper into the teaching of the Presbyterian faith. There is no secret door that holds our deep mysteries. What Reformed and Presbyterian persons and churches believe is public information, available for all who would be interested in examining the teachings and principles of our church.

There is an evangelistic component to this as well. Any Presbyterian can open the *Confession of Faith* and show a friend or loved one what he or she believes about a host of theological subjects. This honesty, mingled with proclamation, is of great value to all who would call the *Westminster Confession* his or her own.

Although there is a great poverty in many churches today, that poverty can be reversed. The poverty is seen in the Rust Belt of eastern Ohio in my friend Paul's journey. He is longing for a confessional church that will teach the truth of God's Word today using the same principles and applications as it will in the next 50 to 100 years. But that poverty is not only in eastern Ohio. There are very few confessional churches in many parts of the world. Yes, this spiritual poverty is seen all over, including where I live. And the poverty is most likely seen in your community as well—many churches, but very few that have much depth or standards of teaching and practice. The poverty has spread throughout all the places where confessional churches once thrived.

What are you to do? Start building trellises! *Espalier* is the answer. Over the next several chapters, we will explore how the Scriptures promote the idea of using a confession and give the church permission to write confessions. We will then take out our toolboxes and build. We will come to see what Westminster confessionalism looks like as it begins to transform your Christian life, your home, and your congregation. We need to rebuild that which has been torn down.

2

THE PILLAR OF CONFESSIONALISM

THE NEWS OF THE FIRE spread nearly as quickly as the fire itself. Thousands upon thousands watched online throughout the day in the middle of April 2019. The famous Notre Dame Cathedral was on fire, and the Parisian fire department was clearly ill-equipped to do anything about it. I checked in throughout the day to see how progress was being made in fighting the fire, but it raged on. The roof and the spire were engulfed, and the hoses, tiny compared to the massive structure, were never able to stretch far enough. The whole world knew what was going to happen.

The spire's collapse was caught on film by an American tourist, and you could hear the gasps coming from the boat where she was recording on her phone. Would anything be left? Would "the Lady of Paris" survive? Most of us watching via the internet, most of those reporting from Paris, and most of the authorities and those on site agreed: Notre Dame was about to become a mere memory.

The too-short hoses continued to spray, the roof eventually collapsed, and the world looked on knowing that the whole building was a loss. A precious part of our shared cultural inheritance was to be reduced to ash by the next morning. The Parisian fire fighters were ineffective.

But despite the odds, we all woke up the next morning to a reality that was hard to understand: Notre Dame had not fallen. The old stone structure (which happens to be the oldest part of the cathedral) was left standing, partly as a skeleton, in the midst of smoldering ash. The stone structure, having stood stalwart in Paris since 1260, remained.

Who knew that Notre Dame would not fall? The authorities did not know. The internet spectators did not know. The Parisians and the tourists interviewed onsite did not know. So who knew? The architects. The engineers. Medieval historians. Notre Dame's structure—around which the roof, spire, and other wood, lead, and copper pieces were built—was made to hold up despite outside dangers and assaults from natural elements. The structure was unmovable. The pillars continued to stand.

Now, you might ask what this Notre Dame story has to do with confessions and being a confessional Christian. Confessions are human documents—documents that are subject to scrutiny, criticism, and challenge. But our confessional heritage, the *Westminster Confession of Faith*, is a confession built not on wood, lead, or other combustible materials. The foundation of the *Confession of Faith* is the pillar of the Word of God.

It has been noted, by those who like to count, that there are somewhere between 1,600 and 2,000 scriptural references within the 33 short chapters of the *Westminster Confession of Faith*. Some may look to the *Confession* and see a magnificent building of men, but when placed under the fires of scrutiny and challenge, what stands forth is that our confessional statements are built on the Word of God—the Bible is the pillar of confessional Christianity.

The confessional Christian must always remember the place of the Bible. When you are hoping to revive your spiritual life, your family's spiritual life, or your church life, confessional Christianity is only able to do so as long as it is founded on God's Holy Word, the Bible. Any confessional believer who is asked, "What is our rule or standard for faith and life?" will answer the same way:

The Bible is our standard.

The Bible is our rule.

The Bible is our foundation.

THE BIBLE'S CHARACTERISTICS

What would you say if someone asked you what the Bible was like? What if they asked you what the best parts—the strongest parts—of the Bible are? The pastors and elders who met at Westminster said:

> The Scriptures manifest themselves to be the Word of God, by their majesty and purity; by the consent of all the parts, and the scope of the whole, which is to give glory to God; by their light and power to convince and convert sinners, to comfort and build up believers unto salvation: but the Spirit of God bearing witness by and with the Scriptures in the heart of man, is alone able fully to persuade it that they are the very Word of God. (*Westminster Larger Catechism*, Answer 4)

In other words, the Bible has many fantastic features, but the fact that the Spirit of God speaks in and through his book (actually sixty-six books) to work out the salvation and changing of sinners is its best feature. The Bible alone tells of the source of humanity's salvation. It is the foundation of our faith, and it drives our lives. In other words, the Bible is the pillar that upholds the Christian faith. The Bible is the pillar of confessionalism, and because of that, it is important that we know what it is about. What are some of the features or characteristics of the Bible?

There are several important Bible features that must be mentioned as we consider the pillar of support in using a confession.

Inspired

When we talk about the Bible, we are not talking about just any book. The Word of God, comprised of the sixty-six books of the Old and New Testaments, has been "breathed out" by God. It can well be argued that the breath of a person is a personal and intimate reflection of his inner health and being. God says in 2 Timothy 3:16 that the Scriptures are "inspired" or "breathed out" by God. This means that, despite the fact that human authors penned the words of the Scripture, their tongues "are the pens of a ready writer" as David says in the Psalms. The Bible is God's Word, and the very breath of God is found with its pages.

Inerrant

Have you ever considered that the Bible was written by so many different authors? The Bible was not written by a committee around a table, but by men from all over the ancient Middle East during different periods of history. And despite this historical truth, the Bible is without error. An Italian theologian who grew up in Switzerland once wrote that the Bible was "kept free from all error . . . truly authentic and divine" (Turretin, *Institutes*, 2.4.5). Contrary to the arguments of those who distrust the Bible, the Bible is without error and without contradiction. It is always a teller of truth.

Clear

For sure, the Bible is not an easy book. The Bible is a book with many words that are "hard to understand," as stated in 2 Peter 3:16, but that does not mean the Bible is not clear in its central teaching: how to be saved and how to live a godly life. The theological word for the clarity of the Bible is *perspicuity*, an unclear word that means "clear." The Bible is clear in its presentation of the law and gospel—the law that condemns man due to sin and the gospel that breathes new life into man through Christ. The simplest of readers can grasp this clear meaning from the Bible. Second Timothy 3:14–15 says that the Bible's teachings are able to make the reader wise unto salvation. We give thanks for the clarity of the Scriptures.

Authoritative

The Bible speaks with the authority of God because it is the voice of God to mankind. Psalm 19:9 says that the Bible is true and righteous altogether. The Bible is the only written word that is able to claim that it speaks with the authority of God. All other written words that are true are only true as far as they reflect God's written Word. This book has the authority to judge the hearts and minds of men and women in a way that no human writing could ever do. "Thus says the Lord" appears over 400 times in the Bible, but it could be written at the beginning of each verse.

Sufficient

We don't need the Bible and ___[INSERT NOUN]___ to inform us what God requires of us in our spiritual lives. The Bible is sufficient. No one can come to you in the name of the Lord and claim that God requires something of you that cannot be proved from the Scriptures. Whether it's making the sign of the cross when praying or celebrating certain saint's days, if it cannot be proven by the Word of God, then it cannot be imposed upon you. The Scriptures alone are enough for your spiritual life's instruction.

THE ONLY RULE

The *Westminster Confession of Faith* opens with statements about what the Bible and its authority is in the life of the Christian and the church. Following a list of the sixty-six books of the Old and New Testaments, the *Confession of Faith* says, "All which are given by inspiration of God, to be the rule of faith and life" (*WCF*, 1.2).

These sixty-six books are the rule for the Christian—in faith and in life. This is the foundation on which our Christian faith—and our *Confession of Faith*—must be built. Question three of the *Westminster Larger Catechism*, a sister document to the *Confession of Faith*, asks, "What is the Word of God?" The *Catechism* answers this question with, "The Holy Scriptures of the Old and New Testaments are the Word of God, the only rule of faith and obedience."

The only rule.

The word *rule* means, "regulations or principles governing conduct; control over (as in a king or queen); or the normal customary state of things." Rules are not just laws, but standards by which we live our lives.

I fly several times a year for work. As a Presbyterian minister, I have board meetings to attend, the regular business meetings of the church (called Presbytery and Synod), and other meetings to which I am transported via the allegedly friendly skies. As I buckle in with the 1960s-style automobile lap belt, I always anticipate the same line from the flight attendant—a line that bothers me tremendously: "FAA regulations require that you obey all of the instruction given by crew members."

Obedience to *all instruction* is the law? What if they ask me to do something such as tamper with the smoke detector? Do I obey their instruction or break another FAA law? When we discuss important matters like being a confessional Christian, we must realize that the *Confession* actually tells us that it is not the final authority we must believe and obey—the Bible is. Unlike the FAA that says you must obey all instruction from the flight attendant, confessionalism begins with this truth: The Bible is your standard. The Bible is your rule of faith and practice as a Christian, and only the Bible is pointed to as our ultimate authority in the Christian life.

Biblical confessionalism is unable to bind your conscience to a teaching that is not found in the Bible. The *Confession* cannot teach something that is opposed to the Word of God or in conflict with the Word of God because, for Presbyterians, the foundation is the Bible alone. The pillar that upholds biblical use of a confession is the Old and New Testaments.

The *Westminster Larger Catechism*, in question three, uses the same language of "rule" that we saw in the *Confession*: "What is the Word of God? The Holy Scriptures of the Old and New Testaments are the Word of God, the only rule of faith and obedience."

Connected to that question are several Bible passages that show the importance of the Bible as the only rule or standard for faith and practice. The pillar of confessionalism is the Word of God; it is these sixty-six books upon which a biblical confession stands or falls. It is important to understand that for the confessional Christian, the Bible is our standard.

The Bible is inspired by God, and it has a purpose for the Christian life. See how the apostle Paul instructs the young pastor Timothy on the value of the Bible in his life: "All Scripture is breathed out by God and profitable for teaching, for reproof, for correction, and for training in righteousness, that the man of God may be complete, equipped for every good work" (2 Tim. 3:16–17).

The profitability of the Bible, besides being the Word of God, is for the Christian's teaching, for reproof or reprimanding, for correcting, and for training for righteousness. The Bible is the standard for all of these things in the life of the Christian. It is our only rule.

When you need to be instructed in your Christian life, where does that instruction come from? The Bible.

When you need to be corrected in your Christian life, where does this correction come from? The Bible.

When you need to be further trained in your Christian living, where does that training come from? The Bible.

It is the standard for you as a Christian—there is no higher authority than the Bible in your Christian life. Not even the experiences that you have are a higher standard than the Word of God.

During a speaking tour of America in the 1960s, a world-famous theologian was asked how he would summarize the millions and millions of words that he had written over the course of his teaching career. The theologian responded, “Jesus loves me this I know, for the Bible tells me so.”

That last phrase is important: for the Bible tells me so. For the confessional Christian, the importance of what the Bible says is to be believed and trusted even above his own experience—even his experience with coming to know and trust in Jesus.

The apostle Peter had an experience with Jesus that is referred to as the Transfiguration. This incredible experience is recorded in Matthew 17, Mark 9, and Luke 9. Matthew writes in verses 1–8:

> And after six days Jesus took with him Peter and James, and John his brother, and led them up a high mountain by themselves. And he was transfigured before them, and his face shone like the sun, and his clothes became white as light. And behold, there appeared to them Moses and Elijah, talking with him. And Peter said to Jesus, “Lord, it is good that we are here. If you wish, I will make three tents here, one for you and one for Moses and one for Elijah.” He was still speaking when, behold, a bright cloud overshadowed them, and a voice from the cloud said, “This is my beloved Son, with whom I am well pleased; listen to him.” When the disciples heard this, they fell on their

> faces and were terrified. But Jesus came and touched them, saying, "Rise, and have no fear." And when they lifted up their eyes, they saw no one but Jesus only.

What an experience! Who would not want to have such an encounter with the Lord Jesus Christ? This occasion of seeing Jesus transfigure—change before his eyes—must have stayed with the apostle Peter his whole life. I imagine it is the type of story that he would share with his children and grandchildren (if he had them). "Grandpa, tell me that story again, the one about Jesus glowing!"

But despite this life-changing experience, the apostle Peter, as an old man, reflected on this experience and his conclusion may surprise you. After reflecting on the transfiguration, Peter says, in 2 Peter 1:19–20:

> And we have the prophetic word more fully confirmed, to which you will do well to pay attention as to a lamp shining in a dark place, until the day dawns and the morning star rises in your hearts, knowing this first of all, that no prophecy of Scripture comes from someone's own interpretation. For no prophecy was ever produced by the will of man, but men spoke from God as they were carried along by the Holy Spirit.

More fully *confirmed*, in Peter's mind, is the Bible—even more than this religious experience on the Mount of Transfiguration. The word *confirm* reminds us of the pillar in its meaning "established and unlikely to change." The Bible truly is the standard—confirmed and without change—for the Christian. This is the standard, not only of doctrine and teaching, but also of Christian experience. Confessional Christians need to be reminded of this and be driven back to the Bible again and again because the Word of God is the pillar of what we profess to believe as Presbyterians. The apostle Paul understood this as he reminded the church in Ephesus that the household of God (the church) is "built on the foundation of the apostles and prophets, Christ Jesus himself being the cornerstone" (Eph. 2:20).

The teachings of the apostles and prophets are the foundation upon which the church is built, and the cornerstone of the building is the Lord Jesus Christ himself. Jesus stands as the center of all that the Bible teaches. We want to see salvation through Christ: Jesus Christ glorified, Jesus Christ as the center of our ethics, and Jesus Christ as the motivation for our being built up. And where do we learn of this Jesus?

Remember that famous theologian on a speaking tour of the United States in the 1960s? "For the Bible tells me so."

The fact that the Bible alone is the standard or rule for the Christian faith reminds you that all things relating to faith and life must be measured according to that standard.

Standards of measurement are important to make sure that you are receiving what you pay for. When you pump gasoline, you can identify the seal that assures you that a gallon paid for will result in a gallon pumped. It is called the Seal from the Department of Weights and Measures. In medieval England, unjust weights and measures would often result in a business owner being publicly flogged for stealing from his customers. Bakers, determined to keep their backsides free of lashings, came up with a way, through the baker's dozen, to assure they were giving the correct measurement to their customers. They over-compensated out of fear of backlash.

The Christian faith is not like this. You are not to over-compensate by believing more than the Bible teaches or requiring more than the Bible teaches in regard to Christian doctrine. The Bible is the true and accurate standard of measurement for all of faith and life. This standard does not require you to guess what you are to believe and do, and it also does not want the standard growing or shrinking—you are to cling to the Scriptures as the measurement of what God desires in your personal Christian life, your family's spirituality, and your church's teaching and practice. The apostle John gives this warning in Revelation 22:18–19:

> I warn everyone who hears the words of the prophecy of this book: if anyone adds to them, God will add to him the plagues described in this book, and

> if anyone takes away from the words of the book of this prophecy, God will take away his share in the tree of life and in the holy city, which are described in this book.

Adding to and taking away from the true standard of the faith results in God's displeasure, according to John. This means that the church should not toss in an extra doughnut; there is no room for the baker's dozen in Christian thought and practice. It means that what is taught and required needs to come from the Word of God. The Scriptures are sufficient. Jesus told a parable wherein he said that even if a man returned from the dead to warn his family of the wrath to come, it would not be enough. Jesus drives his hearers back to the Scriptures.

"They have Moses and the Prophets; let them hear them" (Luke 16:29).

The Bible is enough.

"But," you might ask, "How are you going to sell copies of the *Westminster Confession* if you spend a whole chapter telling people that the Westminster Standards are not really the standard?" That's a great question—and the answer is found in a Latin phrase that you may have heard before:

Sola scriptura.

Sola scriptura means Scripture alone.

IS "SCRIPTURE ALONE" REALLY ALONE?

The idea of *Scripture alone* is frequently misunderstood. The word *alone* seems to imply that there is no other source of information or authority that speaks into the life of the Christian. We know this is not true because the Bible tells us so. There are other authorities in your life. Parents, employers, church elders, the government, and even our *Confession* are all authorities in life. But these authorities must give account to the main authority that God has given to you: the Bible.

This is what *sola scriptura* teaches—the Bible alone is the authority to which all other authorities must give account. Matthew Barrett said it like this:

> Scripture alone is our *final* authority. *Authority* is a bad word in our day of rugged individualism. But the Bible is all about authority. In fact, *sola Scriptura*, means that the Bible is our chief, supreme, and ultimate authority. Notice I did not say the Bible is our *only* authority. . . . Those who sing the mantra [no creed but the Bible] believe that creeds, confessions, the voice of tradition, and those who hold ecclesiastical offices carry no authority in the church. But this was not the Reformers' position. (*God's Word Alone*, 23)

The Scriptures then are the ultimate authority in the life of the Christian, ultimate being the key word. Dr. Joel Beeke, my former seminary professor, uses the word *supreme* rather than *ultimate*, but they basically say the same thing. Speaking of *sola scriptura*, Dr. Beeke says,

> The Holy Scriptures are our supreme and only rule of faith and life; they, not human tradition and reasoning, determine our faith and command our obedience. This means that evangelical theologians are suspicious of fallen reason, so they test their beliefs and practices by the Holy Scriptures. We receive the Bible, not as the word of men, but as it is in truth, the word of God (1 Thess. 2:13)—truthful, uniquely authoritative, and without error. Our minds are servants to receive the Word, not to judge it. The principle of *sola Scriptura* neither rejects Christian tradition nor sets it alongside the Bible as another source of divine revelation, but requires that tradition be tested and sifted by the written Word of God. If God is God, then he is beyond our comprehension and his Word holds absolute authority. . . .
>
> How well do we understand the principle of *sola Scriptura*? Do we search, love, live, and pray over the Holy Scriptures? Is the Bible the compass that leads us through the storms and over the waves we encounter in life? Is Scripture the guide we keep before us always, the rule by which we work? The

> water with which we wash, the fire that warms us, the food that nourishes us, the sword with which we fight, the counselor who resolves doubt and fears, and the heritage that enriches us? (*Reformed Systematic Theology*, 95)

This is where all good confessionalism must begin. The reason we have spent so much time on the Bible in this chapter is to help you understand the authority that the Bible alone has as God's voice to his church—the standard for all faith and life. You need to hear that voice in all places where it is reflected; from the preaching in the pulpit to the pages of the *Confession of Faith*, you need to hear God's voice as the Word is properly used.

As my professor said in his big theology book, it is our rule, our fire, our food, our water, our sword, our counselor, and our heritage. Does the Word of God have this highest place of authority in your life? If it does not, then regaining a commitment to the *Confession of Faith* will not serve your spiritual life in the way that you imagine. But if the Word of God *does* have that place of ultimate and supreme authority, then the pillar is standing strong, and the pillar is able to be built upon.

SO WHAT IS IT—SOLA OR SOLO?

Maybe you're thinking, "If the Bible is clear and authoritative, as you say, and if it is the only rule for faith and life, I still don't understand why I can't study it myself and come up with a solid theology based on Scripture. It seems like different church traditions claim to be based on Scripture, but they teach different things. I think I might feel safer with *solo scriptura*."

One letter can really make a difference. Many of the great debates in church history revolve around one letter changing the meaning of something from truth to error. We need to be careful with our letters.

In the debate around using a confession and the authority of the Bible, we could talk about *sola* and *solo*: only one letter difference, but a world of difference theologically. In the October 2017 edition of *Tabletalk* magazine, Pastor Jason Helopolous wrote on the difference between *sola scriptura* and *solo scriptura* and what it means for the Christian. He said,

> Solo Scriptura advocates a radical individualism that rejects the church, creeds, confessions, and tradition as having any authority while embracing private judgment above all else. This view radicalizes the Protestant ethic and undermines it. Such an approach finds no credence in the teaching of the Reformers or the early church. . . . They viewed an anti-creedal and anti-confessional theology as anti-Christian.

These are strong words, but important when considering big issues like one's relationship to the Bible and the confessional heritage to which we belong. Does the Bible stand as a pillar around which all of our theology grows and develops (*sola scriptura*), or can we rightly make theological statements by just quoting specific verses from the Bible (*solo scriptura*)? Many want to merely parrot some words from the Bible without consideration of the context or the overall teaching of Scripture, but there are many important concepts and teachings that require the reader of the Bible to do the hard work of theology, of looking at the Bible as a whole.

Consider the Trinity. The Trinity is a difficult teaching that is thoroughly biblical, and yet it is difficult to construct a full theology of the Trinity just by opening your Bible and pointing at a text. This is true for our understanding of the Bible itself. Why do we believe that the Bible has authority? Why do we believe that the Bible is inspired by God? Why do we consider the sixty-six books of the Old and New Testaments of equal weight? All of these answers require the Christian to participate in theological discussion and to interact with the history of Christian thought. This is the value of using a confession, rooted in *sola scriptura*.

Solo scriptura says that the individual alone with his or her Bible is more authoritative than the church that is building biblical doctrines around the pillar of the Word of God. One is radical individualism and the other recognizes that the church stands on the shoulders of 2,000 years of theological reflection and biblical studies. Confessionalism stands on the Word alone as the final authority, and even though it may not seem like it, *solo scriptura*, for all of its pious "onlying," leaves the individual Bible reader standing as the true authority and interpreter of Scripture. That is a pillar of self rather than a pillar of Scripture.

I lived a few miles from Universal Studios Hollywood. My family had visited several times—dozens of times, really. One of the high points of our visits was the studio tour. All the tourists pile into a tram and receive a studio tour complete with commentary by some up-and-coming actor wanna-be. One area where filming occurs is called "New York Street." New York Street is a series of building facades that are made out of styrofoam, plexiglass, and other cheap material. Through the magic of film, these buildings look real and impressive, but when one looks closely, they are nothing more than glorified packing material.

This is true in the *solo* and *sola scriptura* discussion as well. *Sola scriptura* may look like just an old building, but under that ancient cathedral are pillars that will not move and will not be shaken. When one looks at the *solo scriptura* position, it may look like a greater reliance upon the Scriptures, but one's own reason, theological presuppositions, and feelings become the structure around which the interpretation is built. *Solo scriptura* may appear to be more relevant, but it is just a facade, much like the sets at Universal

Studios: styrofoam, plexiglass, and cheap materials putting themselves forward as real buildings. *Sola scriptura* is built on the Word of God, *solo scriptura* has merely the facade of the Word. Notre Dame or New York Street. The difference is worth considering.

CAUTION! CAUTION!

Biblical confessionalism is built up upon the pillar of the Word of God. Biblical confessionalism points the believer back to the Word, calls the believer to trust in the Word, and pleads with the believer to know more of the Word. Biblical confessionalism makes the Word more lovely, it makes the Christ of the Word more precious, it makes the truths of the Word more deeply held, and it seeks to elevate God's Word above all else.

But that leaves the reader with a nagging question, and the cynical reader is left with a "gotcha, pastor!" If the Bible is the final authority, and the Bible is central to our spiritual lives, and the Bible is the only written document that can bind our consciences, and if the Bible is the alone—*sola*—that this chapter claims it is . . . then what right does the *Westminster Confession* have to exist? Who exactly gave the church the right to write it? To that question we will now turn our attention.

3
PERMISSION TO WRITE CONFESSIONS

MY MOTHER GREW UP on a small farm in Western Pennsylvania, right outside the Corry city limits. Her parents purchased the farmhouse in April 1952, but the house was already tired and old in the early 1950s. The farm was parceled off from the original farmhouse, an impressive Victorian mansion built in 1870 that sits on an adjacent country road a few acres behind it. The farmhouse that my mother grew up in was a servant's home, according to some, and this house was also built in the second half of the 19th century.

As a boy, I loved visiting Grandpa and Grandma at the farm—seeing the cows, chickens, barn cats, and his prize gobbler named Jake. Any boy would flourish in such an environment. Each of these animals took time to care for, as every farmer knows. As a result, Grandpa and Grandma were not really vacationers; they couldn't be. Cows needed to be milked. The garden needed weeding. Chickens needed to be fed. Bee boxes needed to be cared for. Barn cats needed carp.

Wait.

What?

Carp?

Grandpa often fed the carp from nearby Harecreek to the barn cats as a special treat.

We would put on waders, walk down Scott's Crossing Road, cross the whistling bridge (a bridge that would, due to the surface structure, make a whistling sound when cars crossed over), and make our way down to Harecreek. There Grandpa would take out his fishing spear—that's right, a fishing spear—and begin to watch the carp as they swam.

"You need to watch their shadows," he would say. "The shadows point you to the fish."

When spearfishing, you need to be mindful of light refraction and where the shadow of the fish is in comparison to the body. The science of the whole thing is way above my pay grade, but my grandfather, who quit high school to fight in the European theater during the Second World War, understood what he was doing. When you fish with a spear, you fish by looking at the shadows.

"The shadows point you to the fish." With precision and intuitive scientific ability, Grandpa would spear a few carp, and then we would walk back to the barn to feed the cats. I will spare you the details for now, but fresh carp is quite the treat for barn cats. As a boy who lived in town, I would never forget that sight!

What does this have to do with confessionalism, you might ask?

The "shadows" of confessionalism are in the Word of God. While one might rightly say it is the shadows of confessionalism that lead to the truth and reality of Scripture, I would like to turn that around in this chapter to look to the shadows—the Scripture—to find the reasons to draw up confessions, as well as to provide the foundation for the confessions when they are written. I hope to demonstrate that when one attempts to address current church and cultural issues, the church must turn, not only to specific verses in Scripture, but also to the "good and necessary consequences" of those and other passages, summarizing and systematizing (organizing) Scriptural teaching as a whole.

The church, as you will see, has through Scripture, not only permission, but a warrant, to make confessions. Looking into the depths of Scripture (the shadows in this analogy) points us to the need for confessions, giving the church a warrant to write confessions and providing the foundation for them. As the church formulates confessions, she begins by fishing at the tail and looking to the shadows—the Scriptures point us to the need for confessions and provide the basis for them, much like the shadows of a fish in the creek.

SHADOWS OF THE *CONFESSION*

During the 4th century of the church, a controversy arose around whether Jesus Christ was God. A man named Arius claimed that Jesus was not God, but rather that he was a created being. The church, knowing this was error, called for a council, known now as the Council of Nicea. After condemning the error, a statement—a confession—was drawn up concerning the Trinity and the deity of Jesus. They did what one old writer described as "what common sense and the Word of God had taught the church to do" (Samuel Miller, *Doctrinal Integrity*, 22). They wrote a confession!

He went on to say, "They expressed, in their own language, what they supposed to be the doctrine of Scripture concerning the divinity of the Savior: in other words, they drew up a confession of faith on the subject, which they called upon Arius and his disciples to subscribe."

"Common sense and the Word of God."

What a statement!

What common sense and the Word of God demonstrate is that the shadows of confessionalism are present in the New Testament and the making of confessions is a consequence of, or flows out of, New Testament theology. The New Testament points us in that direction. We see the writers of the New Testament—the inspired writers themselves—setting an example for the church to move in that direction with the doctrine of the church. In the pages below, the New Testament case for using a confession will be made. This confessionalism was not to overthrow the teaching that is found within the Bible, but to summarize it, systematize it (arrange and organize it), and show those willing to hear what the church believes and teaches.

The New Testament was not a time of perfect unity in teaching, even among the leadership. The New Testament has much to say about false teachers and those that were led astray by false teaching. As the New Testament writers responded to these terrible (but normal) aspects of church life, they always pointed their readers to Jesus Christ and to being strengthened in knowing the teaching of the Bible. Theology that is systematized and summarized from the Bible strengthens the church and the individual believer, and it points them to Christ.

STRIVING TOWARD UNITY AND PEACE

The church in Ephesus was struggling in this way. There were false teachers and disunity even to the point where the apostle Paul told the young pastor Timothy to take some wine for his stress-related stomach issues. Timothy needed to relax and reduce his anxiety. In Ephesians 4:2–6, the apostle Paul instructed the congregation toward unity, and this will happen today, as well, through corporate confession of the truth.

The Bible says, "With all humility and gentleness, with patience, bearing with one another in love, eager to maintain the unity of the Spirit in the bond of peace. There is one body and one Spirit—just as you were called to the one hope that belongs to your call—one Lord, one faith, one baptism, one God and Father of all, who is over all and through all and in all."

Notice how Paul says that there is one church, one Spirit, one Lord, one faith, one baptism, and one God and Father. This is a formula, a creed, given to the church to assist her toward a certain goal. We all need goals as we work toward a larger purpose or end. The beach that my family frequented when living in Los Angeles is near the celebrated Muscle Beach where a young Governor Schwarzenegger was discovered by those who would eventually make him famous. Muscle Beach is exactly as it sounds: a beach-front gym where overly-sculpted bodies hang out to show off their strength. In all my years of living there, I was never invited.

The men and women who linger on Muscle Beach do not do so because they are seeking a goal; they have already achieved that goal and are maintaining that purpose. Many hours at the gym and working with personal trainers are what prepares them for Muscle Beach. The work points to the goal. In confessionalism, the apostle Paul encourages us toward maintaining "the unity of the Spirit in the bond of peace." This is the goal: unity and peace within the church. Ephesus was struggling. And how does Paul envision that we reach that goal? It is through the daily exercise of growing in what we know to be true as Christians. The church is called to grow in her understanding of the teaching of the Bible concerning certain topics:

One church.

One Spirit.

One Lord.

One faith.

One baptism.

One God and Father.

This is a confession, isn't it?

It is at least the outline for a confession—it is fishing at the tail and shadows. Paul is asking you as a believer to grow in your understanding of and commitment to these key teachings of the Christian life.

What is the church?

Who is the Spirit?

Who is Jesus?

What is saving faith?

What is baptism?

What is God?

All of these questions have been answered by way of confessional statements. Each of the above questions is answered within the *Westminster Confession of Faith*. When a person says that you need to believe in "One Lord," the believer must then seek the answers concerning this Lord from the pages of the Scriptures. This is fishing at the tail and shadows. This is confessionalism.

SOUND WORDS

Confessionalism means following the pattern of sound words that are found within the pages of Scripture. Not all Christians grasp this concept, but biblical confessionalism requires one to look at and formulate helpful words—sound words—that reflect the theology of the Bible. That's exactly what the apostle Paul says in 2 Timothy 1:13: "Follow the pattern of the sound words that you have heard from me, in the faith and love that are in Christ Jesus."

Another way of saying "pattern of sounds words" is a "form of sound words." The Puritan Matthew Henry saw this as an early statement pointing Christians to write confessions. He says it is

> a short form, a catechism, an abstract of the first principles of religion, according to the scriptures, a scheme of sound words, a brief summary of the Christian faith, in a proper method, drawn out . . .

> from the holy scriptures. (Henry, *Matthew Henry's Commentary on the Whole Bible*, 2019)

The *Westminster Confession of Faith* says, "The whole counsel of God concerning all things necessary for His own glory, man's salvation, faith, and life, is either expressly set down in Scripture, or by good and necessary consequence may be deduced from Scripture" (*WCF*, 1.6). We may deduce from the Scripture that confessions are to be made.

If the apostle Paul and the other writers of the New Testament saw a pattern or a form or an abstract or a brief summary of sound words as being a proper response to trouble in the church, then we must say that the church through the ages has also been called to do the same, in order to uphold the truth of Scripture and protect against error. If it was "common sense and the Word of God" that led early Christians to begin forming confessional statements, then there has been a lot of common sense throughout the history of the church.

Each generation of the church has statements and confessions and summaries of the faith that help believers to understand the Scriptures better. Some of these statements are meant only to speak to a certain generation and a certain issue. For example, within the last couple of years, the "Nashville Statement" on human sexuality was written. This is a statement of sound words summarized from Scripture for a particular time and purpose. And other confessional statements, such as the *Westminster Confession of Faith*, written in the 17th century, are intended to unify churches around the central teachings of Scripture. Both are sound words based on Scripture, but they have different purposes.

TRUSTWORTHY SAYINGS

In other places of the New Testament, we are presented with "faithful sayings"—or some translations have "trust-worthy sayings"—that are "worthy of all acceptance." This formula of "this is a faithful saying" and "worthy of acceptance" reminds us that there are New Testament statements that stand out as mini confessions that all believers should be able to grab hold of and confess, statements that are faithful to the over-arching teaching of Scripture (faithful sayings) and something that the believer holds true for him or herself (worthy of all acceptance).

Think about that. Fish at the tail and shadow of this. If the Bible itself, without summary, was God's intention for the church's theology, meaning that if God did not want the church to write confessions, then why did Paul pull these statements out as faithful sayings that you should know and believe? These faithful sayings are the tail and shadow of the church's positive command to summarize the faith by way of confessions. The "trustworthy sayings" are found in 1 Timothy 1:12–17, 1 Timothy 3:1–7; 1 Timothy 4:8–10; 2 Timothy 2:11–13; and Titus 3:1–8.

Each of these verses that contain the formula mentioned above are verses that the Christian and the church ought to be able to take ownership of and make their own. The woman who led me to Christ used to say, "Nathan, if you can't defend a teaching of Scripture, then you don't own it!" She meant it too; man, do I have stories! In these five faithful sayings, the apostle Paul tells the church to own certain doctrines of the Christian life.

Below you will see each statement and the category of theology that it is teaching. I will not explain the category, but merely state it (you are free to look them up). But the point is clear: the writers of the New Testament would have you accept these statements of faith that are universally acceptable in the church and will prove beneficial for your spiritual life.

TEXT	REFERENCE	DOCTRINE
I Timothy 1:12–17	The saying is trustworthy and deserving of full acceptance, that Christ Jesus came into the world to save sinners...(v. 15).	Doctrine of Salvation
I Timothy 3:1–7	The saying is trustworthy: If anyone aspires to the office of overseer, he desires a noble task...(v. 1).	Doctrine of the Church

TEXT	REFERENCE	DOCTRINE
I Timothy 4:8–10	The saying is trustworthy and deserving of full acceptance. For to this end we toil and strive, because we have our hope set on the living God...(vv. 9–10).	Doctrines of God and Christ
2 Timothy 2:11–13	The saying is trustworthy, for: If we have died with him, we will also live with him; if we endure, we will also reign with him; if we deny him, he also will deny us; if we are faithless, he remains faithful—for he cannot deny himself.	Doctrine of Last Things
Titus 3:1–8	The saying is trustworthy, and I want you to insist on these things, so that those who have believed in God may be careful to devote themselves to good works...(v. 8).	Doctrine of Sanctification

The faithful sayings remind the believer of the importance of taking ownership of the doctrines of the Christian faith.

THE TRADITIONS OF THE CHURCH

The word *tradition* brings different things to different minds. You might think of the traditions that your family has during the holidays, such as which types of pies are served, who hosts which holiday meal, whether turkey, ham, or roast is served, as well as many other things. Each family has their own traditions. The word tradition also might remind you of the song from *Fiddler on the Roof*. "Tradition!"

For many, *that* is tradition: doing what is old or established for its own sake. Tradition may also bring to mind images of military ceremonies such as the changing of the guard at the Tomb of the Unknown Soldier. *Tradition* is a word that is often controversial. What do you mean when you say tradition?

The New Testament uses the word *tradition* in two different ways. In Mark 7:8, Jesus says to the religious leaders of his day that they disregarded the commandments of God so that they could keep the traditions of men. This is a negative use of tradition. But the word is also used positively. In 1 Corinthians 11:2, the apostle Paul says, "Now I commend you because you remember me in everything and maintain the traditions even as I delivered them to you." Tradition as a positive is also used in 2 Thessalonians 2:15 where we read, "So then, brothers, stand firm and hold to the traditions that you were taught by us, either by our spoken word or by our letter."

Tradition in the New Testament can be either negative or positive. The positive use of tradition is in the form of a command. "I command you . . . maintain the traditions." It is also a command that we "stand firm" and "hold to" the biblical traditions of the church. So, tradition *per se* is neither bad nor good; it depends on what the tradition is rooted in. The Scriptures must be the root of the traditions of the church if they are to be valuable for the Christian.

One of the pastors at the Westminster Assembly, Thomas Manton, was a clerk as well as a military chaplain. Speaking of tradition, Thomas Manton said, "Divine traditions are either heavenly doctrines revealed by God, or institutions and ordinances appointed by him for the use of the church. . . . Holding the traditions is nothing else but perseverance in apostolic doctrine" (*Works of Thomas Manton*, 5.488). Manton went on to tell his readers that there are six ways biblical tradition is maintained and upheld in the church (*Works of Manton*, 5.499):

1. The Scriptures themselves are a tradition that the church does not doubt. We stand on this inspired tradition.

2. The facts of the history of Christianity are traditions that the church holds; the virgin birth of Jesus, the miracles of Jesus, and the resurrection and ascension are all factual and historical traditions that are to be upheld for one to call him or herself a Christian.

3. Teachings that are "drawn by . . . consequence from scripture, but are the more confirmed" when we see that the church has held these teachings since very early on are traditions. Manton goes on to cite infant baptism, psalm

singing, and the Lord's Day. These are biblical truths, but the tradition of the church helps us solidify them in the usage of church.

4. Certain theological traditions where the specific words used to describe them are not found in the Scripture, but their teaching is found in the Bible: Trinity, divine providence, and the procession of the Holy Spirit are not phrases you can go to your concordance or Bible app search function and type in. The specific words are not there, but the concepts are found in the Bible and the words have become a part of the tradition of the church (such as the word Trinity).

5. We do not reject the testimony of church history, which shows us that we believe in tradition. Citing church history is citing the tradition of the church.

6. Innocent customs used in the church that are described as "circumstances" tell us that we do not oppose tradition in the church. For example, in my congregation we have worship at 10:30 a.m. and we have Sunday school at 9:30 a.m. One cannot open the Bible and say, "Worship is at noon, thus says the Lord!" You also cannot find a positive command that requires Sunday school. We would call these "innocent customs."

Reflecting on these six aspects of tradition in the church, we see that the church is to hold to the traditions that have been handed down by the apostles. The word *tradition* even comes from the races where a baton was "handed over" to the next racer. We are called to do this in what we believe and practice. This does not mean that the church cannot write statements that reflect what the Bible says; instead, when biblically faithful confessions are made, maintained, and promoted, the traditions of the Scriptures and the apostles are being put forth. Biblical confessions help with the maintaining of apostolic tradition. Of course, the key word in that sentence is *biblical*.

Traditions can be very good. What we believe and practice ought to be rooted in the Bible and able to be seen throughout the history of the church. A useful confession does this.

CONTEND FOR THE FAITH

Jude 3 says, "Beloved, although I was very eager to write to you about our common salvation, I found it necessary to write appealing to you to contend for the faith that was once for all delivered to the saints." Jude's desire is that the church would contend or fight for the faith that was handed down by the apostles. Not all churches are able to say that their theology or doctrine is biblical, apostolic (following the examples of the apostles), or can be traced through the history of the church, but having a confession that is rooted in historic theology is a good beginning!

Occasionally I will look at church websites. I am sure that all pastors do the same. There are two things in the "about us" tab that annoy me on church websites, both relating to a congregation's particular history. The first is when a relatively new off-shoot church makes their history seem as though it is a perfect line between the apostles and the particular congregation being promoted. I don't think that's honest.

The second is when a church says something to the effect that "Our church began when Pastor so-and-so and his wife moved from their city with a vision to begin a church." That may be more honest than the first, but it is a problem nonetheless. The church did not start with you and did not start with your pastor and did not start with your denomination. Honesty in church history is important. Contending for the faith requires that one look to the history of the church—"the faith once delivered" by the apostles—and hold to that as a believer.

In Jude's day there were many false teachers that were denying biblical doctrines of the church, causing controversy, and urging church splits. As Jude called for the church to contend for or fight for the truth as it has been delivered by the apostles, he is mindful that the truth needs to be systematized and summarized to oppose the doctrine of false teachers. The system and summary may change according to the challenges that come before the church, but the truth of the faith is not to change—that is to be a constant in what is delivered to the saints.

BUT SHOULD WE WRITE CONFESSIONS?

Grandpa was very good with the spear, as I said. He rarely missed the fish that he was stalking. I remember as a boy being amazed at the whole tool: the old wooden shaft, the spearhead that was sharp (though clearly ancient), and the old gray rope attached to the end that was used to retrieve the spear from the creek. What was handed down to him from his own father was not merely the tool used for spearing the fish, but more importantly the skill needed to use the tool effectively.

I had to text my uncles and cousins to see who has Grandpa's old spear. Although hunting and fishing are important traditions within my extended family, I was not sure if the tradition of spear fishing continued. In many ways it seems old-fashioned and impractical. My uncle Phil told me that he used to spear carp during spawning season but was unsure where Grandpa's spear went. He assumed it was leaning on a wall in my uncle Bruce's barn. He was right. Uncle Bruce let us all know that it was safe in his barn, although he did not tell me if he ever uses it. The tradition continues, though, with his son, my cousin Craig, who promised to text me some photos of him fishing with it.

We can know the "fishing at the shadow" theory, but should the church write confessions? Looking at some of these important components of New Testament teaching, we attempted to fish from the shadow and tail. We have considered some important statements found within the pages of the New Testament: striving toward unity, following sound words, the five trustworthy sayings, the traditions of the church, and the call to contend for the faith. All of these are important parts of the New Testament that call on the church to write confessions.

Knowing that one needs to fish from the tail and shadow does not mean that spear fishing will continue or that it was ever a practical way to catch fish. Even so, seeing the tail and shadows of confessionalism in the New Testament, one might still ask why the confessions were written to begin with.

A fabric trader from Italy moved to Antwerp, to Zurich, and then in 1592 to Geneva. His fabrics were sought after by many of the wealthy of Europe, and he gained some popularity in various nations because he had moved around so much. Many people throughout Europe remained loyal customers despite his frequent moves. Francesco supported the Reformed church with his wealth. Eventually, he would have a son named Benedict who would travel throughout Europe with him, complete theological training, and become a professor at the Genevan Academy. Benedict's son, no longer connected to the fabric trade, would also be a professor of theology. His name was Francis—Francis Turretin. The high point of Turretin's work in the academy was the writing of a massive three-volume systematic theology. When I say massive, I mean 2,320 pages in English. Massive!

Turretin's style is interesting, maybe learned in part from having a dad who was a theologian but also involved in a trade, or as my kids would say, "he had a real job."

One of the questions that is tucked away in Turretin's massive tome is a question regarding the right of the church to make confessions of faith. He asks whether church "power" is concerned with "doctrines, creeds, and confessions of faith." If you want to find that discussion, it is volume 3, question 30 in the *Institutes of Elenctic Theology*. I struggle even to pronounce the word elenctic!

Turretin begins answering this question with a negative statement. The church is not called to take authority away from the Scriptures by giving the Bible's authority to the church—or by giving the Bible's authority to the particular confession being written. This is not part of what writing a confession is about.

However, the church does have a right to make confessions, in part because the Scripture is a "sacred deposit entrusted to her." The apostle Paul says that the church is a strong foundation of truth (1 Tim. 3:15), and this means that she is to proclaim what the Scriptures teach and use the Scriptures for their purposes. Maybe having a business-owning father helped him understand the "deposit entrusted" concept. A deposit is supposed to bring interest and grow in value. The Scriptures are already perfect and don't need to grow in value, but those who are investing in them grow in knowledge and grace through the study of Scripture.

The church is not only to have these Scriptures as a private book, correcting the errors of private persons, they are public statements and are to be taught. The Scriptures bind the hearers to the truths confessed.

From these points, Turretin argues that "to this power belongs the making of . . . confessions, which . . . preserve the unity and agreement of faith and reject error." This is what Turretin saw as part of the power of the church—the church *has the right* to do it. He also saw that it was part of the "custody" of the church—the church *ought* to do it. The church ought to write confessions for the sake of the custody given to her. We are, according to 1 Timothy 6:20, to guard the deposit entrusted to us.

Why ought the church to write confessions? Because the church is called to strive toward unity, the church is called to promote sound words, the church has been entrusted with trustworthy sayings, the church has traditions to defend, and the church is called to contend for the faith once delivered. Turretin said that these "ought to be valued very highly by the pious. Both because they contain the sum and foundation of Christian doctrine and are like barriers against the errors and corruptions which can injure religion." Confessions are to be written by the church—and treasured by the Christians who benefit from them.

But that does not mean it should not be without warning. Life is full of warnings. Spear fishing came with warnings from my grandfather, from showing care to not get a splinter in my finger from the shaft, to being cautious of the rusty spearhead's dangers, to being tough in the midst of the "ick factor" of watching the carp be slit open and tossed before the barn cats. (Did I say I was going to spare you that detail?) Life has warnings.

The warning that Turretin gives is that confessions "do not have the same authority as the Scriptures, since they must be compared to them and corrected by them." Confessions hold weight only as far as they are biblical in what they teach. Later in the answer, he says that the Bible is the rule, and the confession is the thing ruled. "They are at best secondary rules of doctrine received in any church, since from them can be seen and decided what agrees with or what differs from the doctrine of the church."

The confession, when held under the Scriptures in the heart and mind of the believer, is able to articulate what a church believes, fights for, and contends for: the truth, free of distraction, danger, and dissent. If the believer can heed the warning and use confessions properly, he or she can see that they are, in the words of Turretin, "formulas of agreement and a bond of saving union by which all the pious might be held together in one body and so all distractions, dangerous dissents and schisms, wounding the truth and unity of the church might be shunned."

This is the purpose of the *Westminster Confession of Faith*. What do biblical Presbyterians believe? What do you believe concerning God and concerning Jesus and salvation and the church? It's all laid out for the world to examine—and the intention is to both uphold historic Christianity and to fight against error and distraction, striving toward unity and truth.

This was always the intention of the writers of the *Westminster Confession of Faith*, writers from multiple nations who were called together to answer the questions of what we believe, how we are to worship, and how the church is to be governed. These men knew their permission to write confessions—and write they did. To that story we now turn our attention.

4
THE PICTURE OF OUR *CONFESSION*

THE POSTER IS OF A YOUNG SOLDIER dressed in the typical United States uniform from the Great War with a bayoneted M1930 Springfield bolt-action rifle on his shoulder. He is leaning back slightly with what appears to be a smile on his face and in his arms is a pile of 28 books. The caption reads, "Books wanted for our men in camp and over there. Take your gifts to the public library." Charles Buckles Falls was the artist that designed the famous poster, and it is really the nerdiest of the propaganda posters that I have seen. A copy of it is framed in my family room.

Other of Charles Buckles Falls' posters admonish young men to join the Marines or to sacrifice in various ways for the wartime efforts. Propaganda posters have always intrigued me some, and something that I have noticed, especially in World War I posters, is that the war is depicted as a religious exercise, not merely a national one.

For example, crosses, crucifixes, Bible verses, images of pastors and priests, and other religious iconography appear on several of the posters that I have seen. In many ways World War I was a religious war. One author has argued that World War I became a "religious crusade." World War I was not the only religious war in the history of wars; many wars and scrimmages between nations have had a religious component. As we consider the writing of the *Westminster Confession of Faith*, intended to unify nations and religious practices, we must begin with the fact that the *Confession* was written in the context of civil war and national unrest. How and why did a church write a confession of faith in this context?

OF VANDALISM AND DIVORCES

I pastor an urban church in downtown Orlando and previously pastored near downtown Los Angeles. Urban churches frequently have to clean up trash on their property and sometimes paint over graffiti written on doors and walls. That's a common occurrence with urban churches; vandalism and graffiti are part of life in the big city. During the late Middle Ages, writing on doors was a common occurrence as well, but it was not the same thing. We might say that "the church got nailed" when talking about vandalism, but in the late Middle Ages a church could get nailed as well. Discussion points were often nailed to the church door by those who wanted to provide information, challenge ideas, or seek a debate.

One such occurrence was on October 31, 1517. Martin Luther nailed what he called the *Ninety-Five Theses* to the church door in Wittenberg, Germany, in hope of starting a debate. And what a discussion he started! This was the beginning of what is called the Protestant Reformation, protesting the Church of Rome's understanding of salvation, the doctrine of indulgences, and several other teachings. Martin Luther nailed his *Ninety-Five Theses* to that door in the hope that the German church would begin to debate some of the theological issues of the day. One church historian wrote:

> Armed with his newfound understanding of faith, Luther began to criticize the theology of indulgences in his sermons. His displeasure increased notably in 1517, when the Dominican John Tetzel was preaching throughout much of Germany on behalf of a papal fundraising campaign. . . . Tetzel boasted, he would provide donors with an indulgence that would even apply beyond the grave and free souls from purgatory. 'As soon as the coin in the coffer rings,' went his jingle, 'the soul from purgatory springs.'

> To Luther, Tetzel's preaching was bad theology if not worse. He promptly drew up ninety-five propositions (theses) for theological debate and October 31, 1517, following university custom, he posted them on the Castle Church door at Wittenberg. Among other things, they argued that indulgences cannot remove guilt, do not apply to purgatory, and are harmful because they induce a false sense of security in the donor. That was the spark that ignited the Reformation. (Shelley, *Church History in Plain Language*, 250)

Luther began to question some of the teaching of the Roman Catholic Church, causing division, as well as reformation in the understanding and application of the gospel. The gospel divides. Jesus told us that. That Reformation led to the largest schism in church history since the Eastern and. Western churches divided in 1054. The split was not intentional. Many of the Reformers, including Luther, sought to change the Roman Catholic Church from within, but it was clearly not going to happen. The old church had dug in its heels. One by one, nations throughout Europe were confronted with the gospel and the question of whether to stay in the Roman Church or to do something different. Concerning teachings on the person of Christ, the sacraments, church government, among other things, Lutherans went in one direction and another branch of the Reformation, the Anabaptists, went in another. The Reformed branch, following the lead of men like Zwingli and Calvin, went in yet another direction. Of course, there was overlap; someone with more skill than I have could make a Venn diagram of the Reformation showing the overlap and differences, but one thing was clear: the gospel was recovered and the church had a new-found zeal for both purity and faithfulness.

The *Westminster Confession* was written in England amid a clash within this world of reformations. Should England go this way or that way? Should she pull left toward the Puritans or pull right back toward Catholicism? The national religion was not left up to the consciences of the individual. A king or a queen made religious decisions on behalf of individuals. This is the context of the Westminster assembly.

Welcome to early modern England; we've got royal problems.

ROYAL PROBLEMS

Going back a century, Germans largely followed Luther. Eventually they would create the *Augsburg Confession* that would solidify the standards of Lutheranism in the world. The Dutch and German Reformed had the *Belgic Confession*. Eventually, another church controversy in the Netherlands would lead to the *Canons of Dort* being added to their confessional documents. But England was different. England was a place of theological conflict; many wanted to follow what became known as the middle way—the *via media*. The middle way at times appeared as Catholicism and at other times it looked like a vibrant Reformed theology. What was it? It was a royal problem: the religious atmosphere of the nation largely depended on who sat on the throne. Let's take a century-and-a-half journey through the royal courts to the *Westminster Confession*.

Henry VIII

You may know the story of King Henry VIII, or at least the child's poem about his wives:

> Divorced, beheaded, died:
> Divorced, beheaded, survived.

The story of the English Reformation begins with Henry, who reigned from 1509 to 1547, so the story of the *Westminster Confession* begins here as well. Scottish Presbyterianism was also birthed out of the Reformation in England. Henry VIII began the story with a desire for a son—an heir—and that desire for an heir led to an appeal for annulment, which would invalidate his marriage: essentially a divorce without calling it a divorce. In those days monarchs had to ask the Pope for an annulment. The Pope denied the request and, as a result, the Act in Restraint of Appeals occurred in 1533. This act basically was a way of telling Rome that England was not interested in Roman interference in English church matters (for most people, annulment and divorce were church matters until recent history). The Church of England was now under a new head: Henry VIII. England was now Protestant.

Edward VI

Following the death of Henry VIII, his son Edward VI took the throne. Edward was the son of Jane Seymour, Henry's third wife, and was only nine years old when he began to reign in 1547. Protestants, who desired greater conformity to better examples of Reformed churches, were interested in influencing Edward. Those who wanted the Church of England back under the Pope's authority were also interested in Edward. As Edward went, so went England.

Calvinistic influences won the day. Edward's teachers and tutors, Edward Seymour and John Dudley, had been influenced by John Calvin's theology. Through the influence of these teachers, the church in England took on a more Calvinistic flavor. The *Thirty-Nine Articles of Religion* became the confession of the English Church. Archbishop Cranmer, who wrote the *Articles of Religion*, also wrote the *Book of Common Prayer* that would become the centerpiece of English religion. Reformation was underway under

Edward VI, called by some a new Josiah, after the young Reformer-king of the Old Testament. Foxes' *Book of Martyrs* was published with woodcuts of young King Edward piously sitting at the feet of Reformed preaching.

There was great hope for England to be a Reformed light on a hill to all of Europe. Refugees exiled for the Reformed faith poured into England for respite. Edward, full of hope and the Reformed faith, was proving to be the vessel of God's blessing for reform. But as a teenager, he became very sick, diagnosed with a tumor in his lung. His doctor reported that "the matter he ejects from his mouth is sometimes colored a greenish yellow and black, sometimes pink, like the color of blood." Slowly Edwards legs swelled, and he was unable to rise from bed. He was sick beyond aid. On July 6, 1553, at the age of fifteen, Edward turned to his tutor and said, "I am glad to die" as he entered the presence of his God. Before his death, he willed the throne to his cousin, Lady Jane Grey, a godly young Protestant woman.

Mary I

Following the death of Edward, Lady Jane Gray was proclaimed queen by Edward's counselors. They feared the next in line—a staunch Roman Catholic with family in Spain, the most militantly Catholic nation in Europe. Despite the efforts of Edward's politicians, Protestantism was at risk in England.

Dysfunctional families have consequences. Remember the poem for Henry VIII? "Divorced, beheaded, died . . . ?" His first wife, Catherine of Aragon, had given birth to Mary, the daughter that was not a son. Catherine and her daughter Mary were sent into isolation after the divorce. Lady Jane Grey ascended the throne, but after only nine days, Mary saw to it that she was deposed and beheaded. Mary then took the throne. She was nicknamed Bloody Mary, earning the nickname by executing well over 300 Protestants during her five year reign (1553–1558).

This rage of Bloody Mary caused many Protestants to flee to Geneva, Switzerland, and other Protestant realms. English exiles flooded the continent. Of those Protestants who remained, many died—Hugh Latimer, Nicholas Ridley, and Thomas Cranmer (known as the Oxford Martyrs) being three of the most famous.

Mary's reign did not last long. She died in 1558. Her half-sister Elizabeth took her place, once again changing the religious landscape of the nation.

Elizabeth I

Protestantism was once again the established religion of the land under Elizabeth's reign, which lasted from 1558 until the beginning of the 17th century in 1603. A few years prior, fiery John Knox wrote a book against Mary Queen of Scots, scorning female leadership in the state. Elizabeth, the Protestant, was not the target, but the name calling and misconceptions of women at the pen of Knox never sat well with Elizabeth.

Women were filled with stinking pride. Women dressed to allure the eyes of men. Women were obsessed with sex.

The book did not go over well, as you can imagine. Knox himself said that no other of his books had "greater odium." In other words, it was hated. John Foxe said that it was received with "rude vehemency." John Calvin said it was "somewhat harsh and should be handled with caution" (*Works of Knox*, 4.359).

Elizabeth never forgot the book. She didn't forgive, either. As Protestantism was reestablished in the nation, those who were closely connected with John Knox—some of the most important English pastors and theologians—were not given prominent positions within Elizabeth's court. Elizabethan cancel culture was in full force and the hope of Edward's Reformation grew dim. Protestantism would have to be the middle way—the *via media*—rather than the way of Geneva or Edinburgh.

Under Elizabeth, uniformity was required. The *Prayer Book* was required in the churches, bishops remained in power, and the psalms, the *Geneva Bible*, and the Presbyterian form of government were all suppressed. Presbyterians were forced underground and many who did not want to conform to Elizabeth's rules were removed from their pulpits. Up to one-third of the ministers in England were removed from their pulpits in one day. England would have Protestantism, but Presbyterianism was not going to be it.

James I

Elizabeth died without a husband or child to succeed her, so the winds of religious life shifted again in England. James I (named James VI in Scotland) took the throne of England in 1603. James was the great-great grandson of Henry VIII and was already King of Scotland when Elizabeth died. When he took the English throne, he began a reign over three lands—England, Scotland, and Ireland—essentially reigning in each nation independently.

James was raised a Presbyterian and many in England had hopes that the Presbyterian underground would be able to come out of the darkness as the religious victors this time. Not only was James raised a Presbyterian in Scotland, he also was something of a theologian himself, but not of the Puritan stream that was slowly gaining powerful allies in England.

James wanted to preserve the power and status of his crown. He wrote the *True Law of Free Monarchies*, a theological defense of the rights of kings. The *Geneva Bible* was a translation that promoted the Presbyterian ideals—doctrine, government, and worship all coming from the Scriptures—and a robust Calvinist theology. The *Geneva Bible* was a mine field of a translation, and James understood that. In order to suppress this ever-popular translation, along with other stated and commendable purposes, a new translation—an authorized translation—was made for the churches of England. The *King James Version*, or *Authorized Version*, was completed in 1611. Another wise political-theological move of James was to send a delegate to the Synod of Dort that was meeting in the Netherlands at that time. In this way, James was able to make important political allies.

In his twenty-two-year reign, James was able to maintain a Protestant England, promote Calvinistic doctrines of salvation, keep Presbyterians at bay, and have a Church of England that promoted the royal agenda. But, under the surface, Puritan pressure was beginning to bubble up.

Charles I

James was politically savvy and educated in doctrine. When he died in 1625, his son Charles took the throne. Charles was not James, and Charles was considered suspect by the Presbyterian underground because he married a French princess with a host of Roman Catholic priests at her service. But the princess was not the biggest of Charles's problems; the new bishop was. Archbishop William Laud was something of a tyrant. One historian notes:

> Up to 1630, the Church of England was dominated by Calvinists. . . . Under Charles, such people were side-

> lined, high churchmen were promoted, and the active persecution of Calvinists was begun. . . . As late as 1624, the House of Commons accused him of popery. Yet in 1628 Charles appointed him [Laud] archbishop of York, the second-highest church benefice. . . . Calvinist academics at Oxford and Cambridge were required to rein in their teaching. Later that year, Laud . . . put an end to Calvinist preaching. . . . Soon Laud was elevated to [Archbishop of] Canterbury, having recently condemned the Calvinist . . . articles. . . .
>
> Laud required absolute submission to the king, extending to acceptance of every detail of church ritual. He introduced genuflecting, called the communion table an altar, and banned publications. (Robert Letham, *The Westminster Assembly*, 23–24)

All of this conflict between Presbyterians and those who preferred the higher church model being promoted by Laud was coming to head. In 1640, Charles attempted to impose English ceremonies on the Scots up north. Conflict, controversy, unrest, and unhappiness was the English way of the 1640s. Charles had backed himself into civil unrest. England was at war.

Some men in Parliament, primarily Presbyterians, and the cavaliers who supported the king would go head to head in a civil war that would last for the next nine years.

But we need to pause. We will come back to Charles, but it is important to understand how the Scottish church got involved in an English civil war. It's complicated.

The Scottish Reformation

We have seen conflict in England that follows the throne.

Catholic.

Protestant.

Catholic.

Protestant.

Protestant.

Civil War.

Reformation—or lack thereof—followed the throne. The Reformation in Scotland was what we might call a grass roots movement. The people were reforming and Reformed and that worked its way to the top. Let's take a few steps back 120 years to see how the Reformed faith developed in Scotland.

Luther nailed the *Ninety-Five Theses* to the door in Wittenberg in 1517; a decade later, the Reformed faith had become a part of the intellectual and spiritual discussions of everyday people all over Europe. Like young people today discuss music and other forms of entertainment, theology was discussed in the universities of early modern Europe. Within this decade of intellectual discussion, these new ideas attributed to Luther made their way to Scotland.

A young man named Patrick Hamilton went to study in Belgium, and while there, he learned the new ideas of the Reformation. When Hamilton returned to Scotland, he took up a professorship at St. Andrews University, which was a baston of Roman Catholicism. Hamilton taught this new Reformation theology and eventually wrote a book called *Patrick's Places*, a theological defense of the early Reformation faith (called the Law-Gospel distinction). Hamilton escaped to Germany after being condemned by the Archbishop Beaton. This was in the 1520s.

Eventually he would return to Scotland and stand trial for heresy.

Guilty.

He was executed the same day in which he was condemned. Many thought he would avoid death by returning to the Roman Catholic faith. John Foxe said, "They soon found themselves mistaken." Foxe would record his execution in the *Book of Martyrs*:

> When he arrived at the stake, he kneeled down, and, for some time prayed with great fervency. After this he was fastened to the stake, and the [sticks] were placed around him. A quantity of gunpowder having been placed under his arms was first set on fire which scorched his left hand and one side of his face. . . . He called out with

> an audible voice, "Lord Jesus, receive my spirit! How long shall darkness overwhelm this realm? And how long wilt thou suffer the tyranny of these men?"

This execution rocked Scotland. The people paused and considered the value of that for which Hamilton gave his life. One Catholic said, "The smoke of Patrick Hamilton hath infected all those on whom it blew."

The winds of reformation were blowing. George Wishart, a son of Scotland, studied at Cambridge and came to know and love the Reformed faith. He left Cambridge to return to Scotland in 1544 where he began to be an itinerant traveling preacher. His preaching was received well by some and was offensive to others. East to west, throughout Scotland, he preached and preached—Montrose, Dundee, Edinburgh. The gospel was going forth, and the winds of reformation continued to blow. According to John Foxe, Wishart preached through the book of Romans "with such grace and freedom, and greatly alarmed the papists!"

Wishart was a popular preacher in Scotland. Many were converted, none more famous than the young John Knox.

Despite the many conversions under Wishart's preaching, Archbishop Beaton was committed to seeing him condemned as a heretic. Eventually Wishart was captured. John Knox was with him the night of his arrest and was willing to go with him, but Wishart, his mentor, said, "No, return to your children, one sacrifice is enough."

George Wishart, in his early thirties, was condemned to die for proclaiming the Reformed faith in 1546. Beaton got his way and convinced a noble to hand over Wishart to be tried as a heretic. Of course, he was found guilty as charged—he would be hanged on the first of March.

As Wishart approached the gallows, he preached free grace to his executioner and asked God to pardon those offenders who persecuted him.

The hangman fell to his knees sobbing, "Sir, I pray you to forgive me, that I am not guilty of your death."

Wishart responded, "Come here."

When the hangman came near, Wishart kissed him on the cheek and said, "Here is a token that I forgive thee."

He was hanged and his body then burned on March 1, 1546, at St. Andrews, not far from where Patrick Hamilton was martyred a few years earlier. Wishart's death would cause such an uproar in Scotland that the archbishop who condemned him for heresy, David Beaton, would be murdered two months later in his bed at St. Andrews Castle. Beaton's last words were, "Alas! Alas! Slay me not, I am a priest!"

Contrast his plea with Wishart's last words: "I forgive thee."

Wishart's death caused many in the nation to consider whether his preaching was legitimate. Was the Reformed faith true? Was this minister murdered unjustly? The people of Scotland—from Dundee to Edinburgh to Montrose—responded to Wishart's gospel; the Reformed faith began to burn throughout Scotland.

After Beaton was assassinated in his bed, dozens of Reformed nobility and armed men stormed the castle and kept St. Andrews under siege for eighteen months. A young John Knox, not a participant in the siege but sympathetic as a convert under Wishart, stormed into—yes, into—the besieged castle. Those who were fighting for the Reformed faith deserved preaching and deserved to be catechized, so Knox got into the castle with them.

After eighteen months, the French military sent in a fleet of ships and retook the castle. The Protestant men who had occupied it earlier, including John Knox, were captured and then enslaved on galley ships. Knox rowed as a galley slave for nearly two years. Upon his release or escape (historians are not sure), John Knox was a refugee.

John Knox grew in his understanding of the Reformed faith during these years. His time in England led to a cross pollination between the Scottish and English Reformations. When Mary took the throne from Lady Jane Grey, who was on the throne for nine days after Edward VI, Knox fled to the continent. He spent time in Geneva, Switzerland, ministering to the English-speaking refugee church there. He also spent time in Frankfurt, Germany, as a minister to refugees.

Eventually he would return to his wife Margery—and to his native land, Scotland.

The Reformed faith flourished in his native land. Knox prayed, "Give me Scotland or I die!" Within a year, the Scottish church was writing the *First Scots Confession* and the church had begun to organize by presbyteries. By 1561 bishops were removed.

Scotland was Presbyterian.

Then, for nearly eighty years, Scottish prayers would ascend for reformation in England.

The desire for English piety to be implemented in Scotland was also being prayed. England sought to impose the *English Prayer Book* and the "middle way" of reform onto the people of Scotland. Scotland was not interested. On July 23, 1637, a bishop came to St. Giles Church in Scotland and sought to impose the Mass of the Prayer Book onto the worshipers. Jenny Geddes, often described as a "market-woman," yelled from the congregation at the priest, saying (although in Scots), "May the devil cause you colic in your stomach, you false thief: How dare you say the Mass in my ear!" She then threw a milking stool at the priest. Scotland was Presbyterian and even the market-women were uninterested in England's religion being imposed on them.

By the next year, a great revival had spread throughout Scotland and the people of Scotland covenanted—signed a covenant, some in their own blood—that they would obey

God, withstand innovations of worship (such as England had), and promote the happiness of the king and people. The National Covenant of 1638 was signed by many throughout all of Scotland—lords, nobles, farmers, market-women, preachers, lawyers. Scotland was thoroughly Presbyterian and Reformed. This was 1638. Do you remember who was on the throne in England?

Charles I (Again)

Charles I.

King of Scotland.

Lord of Ireland.

King of England.

There were two Reformed churches that had grown separately and grown with different emphases and starting points. Scotland had the *Scots Confession*, a Presbyterian document. England had the *Thirty-Nine Articles*, an Episcopal document. Both churches had Calvinistic influence. Both churches were Reformed, but Scotland more so. Charles was seeking to impose English religion onto Scotland, but Scotland had become the most thoroughly Reformed nation in Europe.

By 1642 England was in the midst of a civil war, fighting, in part, a theological war with lines drawn between Scottish religion and English religion. The reformed leaders referred to as theRoundheads of Parliament needed Scotland's military assistance. Scotland responded (in the Eshelman paraphrase), "If you want our guns you are also getting our pastors."

Solemn League and Covenant

Seeing that covenanting helped the process of reformation, the Scots responded with an offer to covenant with England. Parliament wanted to resolve the religious conflicts within the nation of England and defeat the Royalists. Royalists supported the king and not the Parliament during the English Civil War. The Scots wanted the English to have freedom to worship God according to their consciences and the Bible. The Solemn League and Covenant was signed by the Church of Scotland in 1643. The English Parliament and the Westminster Assembly signed it a month later, also in 1643. By January of the next year, the Scots had sent an army into England and a delegation of ministers and theologians to assist with the Westminster Assembly.

How did we move from guns to pastors? In keeping with the terms of the covenant, Parliament had called the best of theologians, pastors, and elders from around England to come to Westminster Abbey to work on revising the *Thirty-Nine Articles*. Conflicts over religion were going to be resolved once and for all. Parliament intended to change the religious landscape of the nation—making it more Puritan, more Presbyterian, and more Reformed.

The Solemn League and Covenant was designed toward this end. There were six goals outlined in the covenant:

1. Preserve Reformed Christianity in Scotland in worship, discipline, and government, and seek to reform the churches of England and Ireland. This was called uniformity—one Confession, one Directory of Government and Worship, one Catechism.
2. Overthrow false religion and all that "is contrary to sound doctrine." This included getting rid of everything related to "Popery" and "church-government by . . . all other ecclesiastical Officers depending on that heresy."
3. Promote, with "sincerity, reality, and constancy" the "rights and privileges" of the king.
4. Bring to public trial all who are "incendiaries, malignants, or evil instruments" against the cause of Reformation.
5. Keep England, Scotland, and Ireland in "happiness and blessed peace" by unity.
6. Forever bind those who signed it.

This document, meant to reform, unify, and build the church and state in England and Scotland, stood as the cornerstone of the assembly's work, originally only tasked with revising the Thirty-Nine Articles. The Westminster Assembly, which was in session on and off for a decade (1643–1653), examined theological students and produced over 140 papers and documents. The major work of the Westminster Assembly included the production of a Larger Catechism and a Shorter Catechism to instruct those who had made some progress in the faith or those who had made less progress, such as children. They produced a Directory of Church Government, a Directory of Worship, and a Confession of Faith.

More than 100 ministers, elders, and theologians from England and Scotland gathered to write, debate, amend, correct, and present written products to Parliament as "humble advice" concerning the way of religion in the Bible. The English voted, the Scottish commissioners served merely as consultative members with no vote, and Parliament approved or disapproved as the work unfolded.

The *Confession of Faith* they produced during this time of civil war was made up of thirty-three chapters covering the most important aspects of theology: the doctrines of the Bible, God and the Trinity; God's eternal decree, worked out in creation and providence; sin and the fall of man; salvation; the Christian life; worship and the Sabbath Day; marriage and interaction with culture and the state; the church and her powers and limitations; and the doctrine of the last things: death, judgment, heaven, and hell. The final words of the *Confession of Faith* are a heart cry of faith after a decade of work, the pains of civil war, a king who was beheaded, a tyrant Puritan taking office under the guise of "lord protector," and the hope for lasting reform and unity among the churches. "Come Lord Jesus, come quickly. Amen."

To this *Confession* and its rich biblical and theological heritage we now turn our attention.

5
THE PRACTICE OF OUR *CONFESSION*: PART 1

IN THE LAST CHAPTER, we heard the story of how the *Westminster Confession* came to be written. The story of our *Confession of Faith* began with the English Reformation and a king's serial monogamy. Henry VIII wanted an heir—a male heir—and the fact that he was not getting one was, in his estimation, a problem with his wife, not a problem with him. (Modern genetics tells us that the father has more to do with the gender of the child than the mother. This was not known in the 16th century, which led to Henry assuming it was a problem with his wife.)

Henry did not know the facts. He did not seek to know his wives. He did not love his wives as he ought. Husbands ought to know their wives, queens or not. For a husband not to know the woman with whom he shares life and professes to love is foolish. One's profession of love causes growth in knowledge. A husband that does not seek to grow in knowledge and love of his wife is a bad husband at best and, at worst, a fool.

When considering the *Westminster Confession of Faith* with an understanding of this history we explored in the last chapter, it may be difficult to see the *Confession* and its purpose in the light of love and knowledge. A war, two nations, kings, pastors, and elders debating—how is this love? How is this knowledge? Is the purpose of the *Confession of Faith* and the purpose of confessionalism in general merely to be theologically precise, or is it more?

Although theological precision is important, the *Confession of Faith* was not written so Christians and churches that adhere to it could endlessly debate theology, but instead it was intended to be a unifying document. Before chapter 1 even begins, the *Confession* exclaims to the reader, "Agreed upon by the Assembly of Divines at Westminster with the assistance of the commissioners from the Church of Scotland, as a part of the covenanted uniformity in religion . . . "

The aim of the *Confession of Faith* is that believers would be uniform in their foundation of Christian theology. They would then grow in knowledge and love of that theology. It is a guidebook on knowledge and love. Like a wise husband will grow to know and love his wife more, the intent of the *Confession of Faith* is that the church would grow in knowledge and love of God.

As the *Confession of Faith* is opened, studied, and believed, the reader finds an honest summary of what the Bible teaches about God, ourselves, Christ and his salvation, the Christian life, the culture in which we live, the church, and how to die well.

So, is the *Westminster Confession of Faith* merely a guide on how to grow in theological understanding?

No.

While the *Westminster Confession of Faith* does help the reader grow in theological understanding, its primary purpose is to be a means to growing in love and knowledge of God. The poverty of many churches and Christians today is not merely a poverty of theological depth; it is lack of knowledge of and love for the God of the Bible.

Emmanuel recently flew his drone over our church building and then nearby Lake Eola and into downtown Orlando. As the drone hummed out of our parking lot and into the air, I was amazed at the height it could reach and the perspective of "The City Beautiful." Drones show us a perspective that was uncommon a decade ago. We get an overview that we have not before received.

The book in your hands is not a commentary on the *Confession of Faith*, like G. I. Williamson or A. A. Hodge.

We will not go paragraph by paragraph like the Jerusalem Chamber podcast (check it out); instead, this book is more like Emmanuel's drone intended to make the viewer say,

"I want to live in that neighborhood!"

"That's a cool city!"

"Let's vacation there!"

Over the course of this chapter and the next, we will take a drone overview of the *Confession of Faith.* We saw in the previous chapters the *why* and *when* of the *Confession of Faith.* The *what* hopefully will lead to growth in your love for and knowledge of God.

Let's get that drone up!

GOD—TO KNOW HIM AND LOVE HIM

Knowing but Not Knowing

How does a person come to know and love God? What is the foundation of that knowledge? Chapter 1 of the *Confession of Faith* begins:

> Although the light of nature, and the works of creation and providence do so far manifest the goodness, wisdom, and power of God, as to leave men unexcusable; yet are they not sufficient to give that knowledge of God, and of His will, which is necessary unto salvation (*WCF,* 1.1).

People come to know God by the light of nature as creation cries out that there is a God, and he is good, wise, and powerful. Psalm 19:1 says, "The heavens declare the glory of God." But that's not enough. The providences of history teach us about God and his character as well. God is good! God cares for his creation! All cultures are religious; even unbelieving students and scholars of society and culture acknowledge the religious nature of humanity.

But do they know God?

"Of the Holy Scriptures," the title of chapter 1, helps us to understand the paradox of humanity knowing *of* God and yet not *knowing* God. Romans 1:20 claims that much of humanity knows God, but does not know him—they know God through knowledge of his creation even though that knowledge is incomplete, and yet they do not know him experientially—and they are "left without excuse." There is sufficient evidence in creation to communicate much of God's character. But God's Holy Word, the sixty-six books of the Old and New Testament, contain "the whole counsel of God, concerning all things necessary for his own glory, man's salvation, faith and life, is either expressly set down in Scripture, or by good and necessary consequence may be deduced" (*WCF*, 1.6). For those who want to know God, the Scriptures become the source of that knowledge, beyond what we know from creation.

That does not mean that knowing and loving God will be effortless. "We acknowledge the inward illumination of the Spirit of God to be necessary" (*WCF*, 1.6) and "all things in Scripture are not alike plain in themselves, nor alike clear unto all" (*WCF*, 1.7). Difficulties will arise and hard work will be required to grow in knowledge of God, but all things worth learning are worth working for. Remember: math class is difficult.

Who Is God, Anyway?

Having laid the foundation that all Christian belief and practice is to be found within the Word of God, the *Confession of Faith* turns attention to the God of the Bible. "Of God and of the Holy Trinity" begins with a beautiful list of God's attributes or characteristics that often echo the Scripture's descriptions of the God of the Bible:

> There is but one only, living, and true God, who is infinite in being and perfection, a most pure spirit, invisible, without body, parts, or passions; immutable, immense, eternal, incomprehensible, almighty, most wise, most holy, most free, most absolute; working all things according to the counsel of His own immutable and most righteous will, for His own glory; most loving, gracious, merciful, long-suffering, abundant in goodness and truth, for-

> giving iniquity, transgression, and sin; the rewarder of them that diligently seek Him; and withal, most just and terrible in His judgments; hating all sin, and who will by no means clear the guilty. (*WCF*, 2.1)

This is the God of the Bible, the God that the Scriptures want you to know. The *Confession of Faith* lists thirty-five proof texts, or Bible references, that the reader can study to learn more about God and his attributes. What do these attributes mean? Several of these words may require a dictionary, as they are technical terms—jargon—filled with rich theological meaning. "Without passions" may be the one in the list that needs the most explanation. C. S. Lewis was not a Presbyterian or even a theologian; he was an English professor. However, he astutely noted that "the passion of love is something that happens to us, as 'getting wet' happens to a body: and God is exempt from that 'passion' in the same way that water is exempt from 'getting wet.' He cannot be affected with love, because He is love" (*Miracles*, chapter 11). God's attributes make up who he is completely—it's not merely that God is loving; God *is* love. One scholar, reflecting on these many attributes, wrote, "We must be impressed by the fact that the assembly's various references to the love and mercy of God far outstrip any other adjectives or descriptions of God's character" (Chad VanDixHoorn, *Confessing the Faith*, 32).

The "one only, living, and true God" is better known through the following paragraph; but there is more to knowing God than merely knowing his characteristics. A husband's wife is more than just her personality; she is also defined, in part, with what she does—her actions. Similarly, God is known by what he does in relation to his creation:

> All sufficient, not standing in need of any creatures . . . the alone fountain of all being . . . most sovereign dominion . . . his knowledge is infinite, infallible, and independent . . . most holy in all his counsels . . . to him is due from angels and men, and every other creature, whatsoever worship, service, or obedience, he is pleased to require of them. (*WCF,* 2.2)

The God of the Bible is unlike his creatures; he is free and sovereign and perfect. He is able to require worship of his creatures in the manner that he finds best suited to them. But this heady theology did not originate with these chapters. God, known in Scripture, is also the God that the church has professed since the beginning. The writers of the *Confession* did not throw off the history of biblical interpretation in their quest to be biblical. Historic words and phrases help the Christian to understand God's nature and what makes God, God.

Words and phrases such as "three persons," "one substance," "neither begotten nor proceeding," "eternally begotten," and "eternally proceeding" are all used to describe God as Trinity. The God of the Bible, to be known rightly, must be understood and worshiped in unity and trinity. These phrases and words draw the reader back to the rich historical creeds and confessions written as defenses of who God is. The writers of the *Confession* wisely and carefully chose theological language about God that goes back to the mid-300s, with the writing of what is called the *Nicene Creed*.

God as Sovereign

God's character, God's relationship with his creation, and God's relationship with himself summarize chapter 2 of the *Confession of Faith*. To know God, we must look to the Scriptures, and from the Word, we come to know God.

But God is not silent in this world or its affairs. God has spoken and sovereignly governs all things. "God, from all eternity, did, by the most wise and holy counsel of His own will, freely and unchangeably ordain whatsoever comes to pass" (*WCF*, 3.1). As the reader seeks to know God according to the Scriptures, several questions come to mind for the discerning reader, especially in light of a God who is totally sovereign. He's in charge. There's no contest.

For the new disciple, or the person learning about Reformed theology for the first time, the idea that God is sovereign can be disturbing. There can only be one king, and the idea that God is in charge and I am not can be difficult for the new believer. Consider the famous gospel tract that many new believers have had to wrestle through: the image of a cross being placed on a throne as the new believer takes his new place off the throne! Deep down, we want to be the ruler of our own lives. But we have been dethroned! Each of us has to wrestle with the concept of God's eternal will.

The Decree of God

As the *Confession of Faith* discusses the decree of God, we see that soul-searching questions are answered throughout the short chapter. You could imagine the conversation between the disciple and his mentor going something like this:

Disciple: "If God is sovereign, then sin must come from God—is this his fault?"

Mentor: "No, 'God is not the author of sin'" (*WCF*, 3.1).

Disciple: "Well, if he's not the author of sin and he's sovereign, it seems that human liberty is taken away from us."

Mentor: "God does no violence to the will of humanity. There's still contingency and second causes and liberty; these things are established because God is sovereign!" (*WCF*, 3.1).

Disciple: "Maybe his sovereignty is best understood as though God looked down the corridor of time and called that his will. Is that how to understand this?"

Mentor: "No, God's knowledge or decree does not depend upon him foreseeing the future choices of man. That's not it!" (*WCF*, 3.2).

Disciple: "Well, if it's not connected to the future, can men change the decree of God?"

Mentor: "The decree cannot change, whether that attempt is by men or angels" (*WCF*, 3.5).

Disciple: "If God determined who can be saved, does he also determine how that person will come to be saved?"

Mentor: "Absolutely!" (*WCF*, 3.6).

Disciple: "So does that mean that the number of people that God saves is already determined, or should I say, decreed?"

Mentor: "Yes, the Bible teaches that God withholds mercy as he pleases" (*WCF*, 3.7).

Disciple: "These are very powerful truths taught in the *Westminster Confession of Faith*. Maybe we should yell these from the rooftop! Everyone should know about God's predestination and the work!"

Mentor: "Listen to how the chapter on the decree ends: 'This doctrine of this high mystery of predestination is to be handled with special prudence and care'" (*WCF*, 3.8).

Knowledge of God requires the believer to dive into the Scriptures and to see his attributes, his relationship with creation, his triune nature, and his work. He is at work in the realm of creation and specifically on behalf of you and me.

This is where the *Confession of Faith* takes us next. We not only are called to know God, but we are also called to know ourselves.

WHO AM I? WHERE DID I COME FROM? WHY AM I HERE?

Where did I come from? What is the purpose of this life? The creation is briefly discussed in chapter 4 of the *Confession of Faith*; we note a few important phrases. God made the world "out of nothing . . . in the space of six days" (*WCF*, 4.1). The *Confession of Faith* takes a stand on creation in promoting the clear teaching of Genesis 1–2 that the world was not created out of previously existing matter, but instead was created "out of nothing" in six literal days. During the time of the writing of the *Confession of Faith*, popular creation doctrines included both the idea that the world was created instantly, the creation was eternal, or the idea that the creation was created over long periods of time. "Out of nothing" and "in the space of six days" both turn the disciple back to the Scriptures rather than popular theories that point away from the Scriptures.

We are also told that both Adam and Eve, our first parents, were made in the image of God, "with knowledge, righteousness, and true holiness" (*WCF*, 4.2). Humanity bears the image of Christ. Adam and Eve enjoyed communion with God and had dominion over the creatures. These first parents, in God's image and without sin, did, however, have the ability to sin and to fall from that place of God's favor. They had the law "written in their hearts, and the power to fulfill it" but they did not keep the command "not to eat of the tree of the knowledge of good and evil" (*WCF*, 4.2). Sadly, with disappointment and consequence—eternal even—our parents ate, and they fell. Darkness, sin, death, and hell came upon our first parents and upon the whole human race.

We will come back to that later, but this question should haunt you, did God leave humanity after the fall?

Did God Leave Us Behind?

Where is God?

I was blessed to be raised in a home with both of my parents. Most of my good friends from high school were not so blessed. Mike's mother had passed away from cancer. Shawn lived with his mother and step-father. Jason knew his dad, but rarely saw him—I never met him once in all our years of friendship. Many of my closest friends had this reality in their lives: parents often leave. Sadly, this affects how we view God, especially when Jesus calls us to pray, "Our Father which art in heaven."

Fathers leave.

So, has God left?

Can we believe in a creation by a good and holy triune God and yet believe that God has left his creation behind to fend for itself? In the words of the apostle Paul, "God forbid!"

God's Providence

Chapter 5, "Of Providence," begins, "God, that Creator of all things, doth uphold, direct, dispose, and govern all creatures, actions, and things, from the greatest even to the least, by his most wise and holy providence" (*WCF,* 5.1). God has not left us to figure things out on our own; he does not allow for us to be self-made or do-it-yourself Christians. He is a God of means, which reminds us that he uses certain things to bring his people to himself. Of course, he is free also to "work without [means], above, and against them, at his pleasure" (*WCF,* 5.3). There are also times when it seems as though God is far away (*WCF,* 5.5), and God's providence is also over unbelievers as they are hardened against him in their unbelief (*WCF,* 5.6).

The Fall Brings Changes

Having spoken of God's providence over his creation—over believers and unbelievers—the assembly next turns to the "Fall of Man, of Sin, and of the Punishment Thereof." As humans, our relationship with God's providential dealings depends on where we stand—on this side of eternity and in the life to come.

A child's relationship with his or her parents changes over time. Little babies are totally dependent upon their parents, needing assistance in even eating and dressing. As children grow into their teens, they begin to assert their independence and eventually (hopefully) move out of the house to begin a life on their own as young adults. Marriage and children normally come, again changing the relationship between child and parent. Eventually parents are the ones in need of care, and the loyal child will take his or her turn in practicing love toward the parent, perhaps even assisting in eating and dressing. Relationships change.

The relationship the Christian has with sin changes over time, too, and this was true from the beginning. Chapter 6 tells us that "Our first parents . . . sinned, in eating the forbidden fruit" (*WCF*, 6.1). We are also reminded that God allowed this sin for his own glory. But what were the lasting effects of this sin upon the race? Paragraph 2 tells us, "By this sin they fell from their original righteousness and communion with God, and so became dead in sin, and wholly defiled in all the parts and faculties of the soul and body" (*WCF*, 6.2). The fall changed humanity. Not only did the relationship with God change, but we see that humanity became "dead in sin" and that the entire person became corrupt in all "parts and faculties of the soul and body" (*WCF*, 6.2).

In Adam, All Fell into Sin

One may argue that just because Adam and Eve fell from their state of being in a right relationship with God that ought not to affect someone else's relationship with God. But, the Westminster divines understood that because of a *covenant* relationship that Adam had with all mankind, "the guilt of this sin was imputed; and the same death in sin, and corrupted nature, conveyed to all their posterity descending from them by ordinary generation" (*WCF*, 6.3). Sin changed all of humanity that would be born of the human race—that is, all those born in the ordinary way. Jesus Christ, not having been born in the ordinary way, was protected from imputed sin and corrupted nature and brought hope into the world that our bondage to sin would be broken.

But for the rest of us, we are told that sin so affects us that we are "utterly indisposed, disabled, and made opposite to all good, and wholly inclined to all evil" (*WCF*, 6.4), that this corruption "remain[s] in those that are regenerated" (*WCF*, 6.5), and that sin "bring[s] guilt upon the sinner" (*WCF*, 6.6). Despite this harmful relationship with sin that corrupts all of us completely, humanity is not left without hope. In our quest to be confessional and to grow in our understanding of what the Bible teaches about how to know and love God, we have been given a view of humanity that is in tension.

We are image bearers of God. We are caretakers of His creation and have been given a mandate to create, work, and think. We were created good. Yet we sinned, and that sin corrupted us wholly.

What is the Bible's answer? Throughout the history of the church, teachers and preachers have given different answers:

We are basically good and need moral reform.

We sin, but we can choose not to if we want.

We are totally depraved, and God must make a way for salvation.

The honesty of confessionalism protects the Christian from having to read between the lines of teachers and preachers. In the 2,000 years since the resurrection, some of the most convincing and charismatic (in personality) of teachers have taught unbiblical views concerning the relationship between sin and humanity. Using a confession protects churches, families, and believers from that error. The errors concerning humanity's relationship with sin results in changes concerning how God saves as well. To know and love God we must know ourselves and the great lengths to which the Lord Jesus went to rescue and redeem a fallen people.

KNOWING AND LOVING CHRIST AND HIS SALVATION

To know and love God, we must know and love that which Jesus Christ has done for sinners. Using a confession keeps us from vague statements about the person and work of Christ; so it protects us from false versions of Christ. The *Confession of Faith* spends many chapters unfolding the Bible's teaching concerning Jesus and his salvation:

God's Covenant with Man, chapter 7.

Christ the Mediator, chapter 8.

Free-Will, chapter 9.

Effectual Calling, chapter 10.

Justification, chapter 11.

Adoption, chapter 12.

Sanctification, chapter 13.

Saving Faith, chapter 14.

Repentance unto Life, chapter 15.

Good Works, chapter 16.

Perseverance of the Saints, chapter 17.

Assurance of Grace and Salvation, chapter 18.

These chapters are rich and will both challenge and encourage you in your walk with Jesus Christ. Confessionalism is that *espalier* tree or trellis upon which your faith will develop and flourish toward maturity in the faith. Connected to the above chapters lie hundreds and hundreds of proof texts or biblical references to examine and consider. I would encourage you to get a copy of the *Confession of Faith* and drink deeply from this fountain of biblical wisdom. This is merely a taste of what's to come.

Covenant of Grace—Jesus Christ Bridges the Chasm between God and Man

"The distance between God and the creatures is so great" (*WCF*, 7.1) that God had to come down to our level by way of covenant for humanity to have any "blessedness and reward" (*WCF*, 7.1) in him. The covenant before the fall was called "a covenant of works, wherein life was promised to Adam . . . upon condition of perfect and personal obedience" (*WCF*, 7.2), but that covenant was broken when Adam sinned.

The Lord made a second covenant, "commonly called the covenant of grace; wherein he freely offereth unto sinners life and salvation by Jesus Christ, requiring of them faith in him that they may be saved" (*WCF*, 7.3). Jesus Christ is the central figure of the Scriptures. If this truth is grasped, it will aid in the flourishing of your spiritual life.

Jesus is so central to the message of the Bible that our *Confession* teaches that the covenant of grace, made with Jesus for the saving of sinners, was "differently administered in the time of the law, and in the time of the gospel" (*WCF*, 7.5). It also teaches that in the gospel, Jesus Christ in the covenant of grace is put forth in the "preaching of the word, and the administration of . . . baptism and the Lord's Supper" (*WCF*, 7.6). Worship, therefore, becomes about lifting up Jesus rather than much of what modern evangelical worship provides for those in the pews. The *Confession* reminds us that this message is all about Christ and his glory. He stands at the center of salvation—in both the Old and New Testaments—and the covenant of grace is a deep and glorious truth that is found throughout all of the Scriptures.

This Jesus, "the Son of God, the second person in the Trinity, being very and eternal God, of one substance, and equal with the Father, did, when the fulness of time was come, take upon him man's nature . . . being conceived by the power of the Holy Ghost, in the womb of the virgin Mary" (*WCF,* 8.2). Jesus lived a perfect and sinless life in this world and died a perfect and sinless death to secure salvation for his people. "By his perfect obedience, and sacrifice of himself . . . hath fully satisfied the justice of his Father; and purchased not only reconciliation, but an everlasting inheritance in the kingdom of heaven, for all those whom the Father hath given unto him" (*WCF*, 8.5).

So what does this reconciliation and everlasting inheritance look like?

It begins with God using the Bible and the Spirit's blessing on sinners, "enlightening their minds spiritually and savingly to understand the things of God taking away their heart of stone, and giving unto them a heart of flesh; renewing their wills and, by his almighty power determining them to that which is good; and effectually drawing them to Jesus Christ; yet so they come most freely, being made willing by his grace" (*WCF*, 10.1).

Justification by Faith

As the will of a fallen sinner has been made willing by God's grace, he or she will be drawn to Christ and be saved.

The theological term for being legally made right with God is justification. Justification happens through "imputing the obedience and satisfaction of Christ unto them, they receiving and resting on him and his righteousness, by faith: which faith they have not of themselves it is the gift of God" (*WCF,* 11.1).

By faith! That's how the believer comes to justification in the words of our *Confession*. "Faith, thus receiving and resting on Christ and his righteousness, is the alone instrument of justification" (*WCF,* 11.2). But this justification by faith will not be alone. It will be "ever accompanied with all other saving graces, and is no dead faith, but worketh by love" (*WCF,* 11.2).

The *Confession* then spends the next several chapters describing in detail what the pastors and elders at Westminster meant when they said "all other saving graces."

Adoption

They begin with adoption, describing how all believers "enjoy the liberties and privileges of the children of God" (*WCF*, 12.1). When one has been saved by faith and adopted as his child, God does not leave the new believer to continue to live in the same way. Just as adopted children often reflect something of their adopted family—manners, ways of speaking, habits—God does not leave his children without that blessing of adoption.

Sanctification and Repentance

The *Confession* teaches us that we are sanctified, or made holy. The *Confession* says, "sanctification is throughout, in the whole man, yet imperfect in this life" (*WCF*, 13.2). Of course, we all know that there are strong Christians and weak Christians. We know believers who struggle in many ways and other believers who seem to have it together. The *Confession* encourages us in this when we look around and seem to come up short. We are kept from discouragement with the understanding that the Bible talks about some who are stronger than others. This is described by the assembly as faith "different in degrees, weak or strong" (*WCF*, 14.3). It goes on to remind the believer that repentance, or turning from sin, is an important component in the Christian life, especially in one's spiritual growth. The *Confession* says, "It is every man's duty to endeavor to repent of his particular sins particularly" (*WCF*, 15.5). Jesus told us to daily deny ourselves, take up the cross and follow him. If discipleship is daily self-denial and daily cross bearing, then repentance is vital to the Christian.

The Place of Good Works

My brother Preston is a fireman and has been for many years. He is a member of the Stanford Hose Company in Corry, Pennsylvania. He has many heroic tales of fighting fires. He promotes all things related to the fire department—

everything except drinking from a fire hose. The power of a fire hose's pressure would overwhelm and not refresh the thirsty. In this overview of the *Confession of Faith*, we have started with the Scriptures and moved to the knowledge of God, which happens through knowing Christ and his salvation. Unlike a fire hose, the *Confession* unfolds all of this slowly, in an organized, sequential way, so that the soul and mind are not overwhelmed, but watered and able to grow.

The goal of salvation is that we will engage in good works, so that we might live according to the profession of faith that we have, to the glory of God. Good works reflect our heart. The *Confession* reminds us that good works are defined for us in the Bible and are not to be done "out of blind zeal, or upon any pretense of good intention" (*WCF*, 16.1). Our good works that flow out of our love for God are "wholly from the Spirit of Christ" (*WCF*, 16.3), and we are reminded that "we cannot by our best works merit pardon of sin, or eternal life" (*WCF*, 16.4).

Even as Christians, we tend to fall back onto the false idea that God's love for us is dependent upon our "being good." The *Confession*, understanding the human heart, seeks to protect the believer from this error. Protection from error aids us in our love for God and helps us to flourish as we rest in him. As we rest in Christ, we will persevere in the Christian life (*WCF*, 17), and we will grow in our assurance and understanding of our place in Christ (*WCF*, 18). All of this is meant to encourage you, to draw you to Christ, to keep you in Christ, to help you flourish as a believer, and to prepare you for the bumps in the road that lie ahead. As you grow in your knowledge and love of God with the help our confessional standard—always with Bible open—you will come to truly see that using a confession is not intended to push you into "traditions of men" but instead to aid in your growth and knowledge of God and his salvation.

Remember that a husband who does not know his wife is not really capable of being a good husband. Both husband and wife will be frustrated, angry, and often disappointed in their marriage. For the Christian who does not take time to know God according to the Bible, he or she will often be frustrated and unable to navigate life. The *Confession of Faith* is a framework for knowing and loving God and an honest and biblical guide for flourishing in the Christian life. And now it is to the Christian life that the *Confession* turns its attention.

6
THE PRACTICE OF OUR *CONFESSION*: PART 2

STORIES OF BELONGING are part of the common human experience. In 1960, P. D. Eastman wrote *Are You My Mother?* about a young egg that hatches and goes on a 64-page adventure attempting to find its mother. A kitten, a hen, a dog, a cow, a car, a boat, a plane . . . "Are you my mother?"

From the moment of hatching, the little bird understood something innately—the need to belong and to identify is part of the experience of existence. God has created us to belong.

There are more serious examples that could be given than Eastman's famous children's book. "Identity" is probably one of the most common buzz words among young adults, finding its way into film, television, and other forms of literary expression and entertainment.

How do you identify?

What's your identity?

These two questions are beyond today's primary identity discussion points of race, gender, and sexual preference. They are questions related to the human experience and the intrinsic need to belong. I doubt that among the bombs and gunfire of the English Civil War the Westminster pastors and elders were sitting around asking about their identity and whether they belonged—but the *Confession of Faith* turns toward identity in its remaining chapters.

When we come to believe in the God of the Bible and the great doctrines of the salvation, there is identity attached to that faith. The apostle Paul describes that faith identity in Ephesians 1 when he says that we are "in him," and because of that union with Christ, we become a part of something bigger. We belong. We are part of the beloved. Our identity is now in Christ.

As a Christian friend from high school would leave his house, his dad would say, "Scott, remember who your Father is." His dad was reminding his son that his identity is bigger than himself. He belonged to something more—someone more, and it wasn't his earthly father. He was a Christian, and being a Christian changes our identity and how we live in this world. Chapters 19–33 of the *Confession of Faith* turn our attention to further practical aspects of the Christian experience.

Chapters 19–22 of the *Confession* show us how to live as a Christian. How do we live as Christians in society? Does the Christian life have anything to say about culture (chapters 23–24)? What is the church, and why is it important to one who is a believer (chapters 25–31)? And as we, as Christians, come to the end of our lives, how do we die well? What are our expectations as we move from this life into the next (chapters 32–33)? These are practical questions that help us as we consider identity.

KNOWING THE CHRISTIAN LIFE

"How should we then live?" Many of you may remember the knickered and white-goateed Francis Schaefer asking that question. How should we then live? The question is one of great importance, and the *Confession* moves from Christ and his salvation (chapters 8–18) to how one who has trusted in Christ ought to now live.

The Beatles, in 1967, sang, "all you need is love." The *Confession of Faith* says that when living out the Christian life, the believer must go back to Adam and remember that "God gave to Adam, a law, as a covenant of works, by which he bound him and all his posterity to . . . obedience" (*WCF*, 19.1). This is what God wanted from Adam—love by way of obedience. Jesus would later say, "If you love me you would keep my commandments." This covenant with Adam, the covenant of works, was discussed in the *Confession* already, but here we are reminded that this law given to Adam comes back to the people of God summarized in the Ten Commandments (*WCF,* 19.2). The "how shall we then live?" of the Christian faith becomes "love is all we need" in living the Christian life. The *Confession* says in 19.2, "the four first commandments containing our duty towards God; and the other six, our duty to man." This is "commonly called" the moral law (*WCF,* 19.3).

"All you need is love" said the Beatles. Jesus said,

> "You shall love the Lord your God with all your heart, with all your soul, and with all your mind." This is the great and first commandment. And the second is like it: "You shall love your neighbor as yourself." On these two commandments depend all the Law and the Prophets. (Matt. 22:37–40)

The Christian life is a life of obedience to God—which is described as love for God and then love for our neighbors. The *Confession* does not spend a lot of time explaining the meaning of each commandment, but that is done in the *Larger Catechism*, another document written by the Westminster Assembly.

The *Confession* does, however, help us to think through categories of law for when we are reading our Bibles. What laws apply to me today? How would God have me live in this world? Am I forbidden from eating a goat boiled in milk? Am I forbidden from mixing polyester and cotton? Am I forbidden from eating . . . wait for it . . . bacon!?

The *Confession*, teaching you how to live out the Christian life as you come to a greater understanding of the Bible, divides law into three categories: moral law, ceremonial law, and judicial law.

The moral law, which is summarized in the Ten Commandments, is the love of loving God and loving neighbor (*WCF*, 19.2).

The ceremonial law includes Old Testament types and shadows, "prefiguring Christ, his graces, actions, sufferings, and benefits." The *Confession* tells us that these ceremonial laws are "now abrogated, under the New Testament" (*WCF*, 19.3). Abrogated means repealed or done away with.

The third category of law that the *Confession* puts forward are political laws that belonged to the nation of Israel until those laws "expired together with the State of that people" and are "not obliging any other now" (*WCF*, 19.4). This means that the laws that deal specifically with the governing of Israel as a nation are expired except for what the *Confession* calls "the general equity thereof may require."

So how do we live the Christian life? We love God and love our neighbor.

What does that look like? We read God's law in the Bible to see how to love and live as Christians.

What laws are to be applied when we think about living out the Christian life? The moral law.

What about those other laws? They are ceremonial or political in nature; they don't really apply to my Christian walk in the same way that the Ten Commandments do.

But someone will say, "We are under grace, not under the law!" The *Confession* helps in our understanding of that as well. These ways we use the law are not "contrary to the grace of the Gospel, but do sweetly comply with it; the Spirit of Christ subduing and enabling the will of man to do that freely, and cheerfully" (*WCF*, 19.7).

This is foundational to the practice of our *Confession*. We are taught that the law has a place in knowing the Christian life, and the keeping of the law—freely and cheerfully—is a reflection of love.

Living in Christian Liberty

The law-and-love discussion can lead to extremes. You have met Christians who want to impose things not found in the Bible upon other Christians. Sometimes that is to make sure that God's law is respected and other times it is because "this is how it has always been done." Whatever the motivation, this is not what the Bible tells us to do. The Westminster Assembly understood this problem that is within the heart of humanity. Boundaries make us feel safe—but can we go too far? Of course.

Christian liberty (our freedom as believers) follows the *Westminster Confession*'s discussion on the law. Law and liberty go together and should not be separated. The Christian is free from the guilt of sin (*WCF*, 20.1) as well as free from the ceremonial law's requirements "to which the Jewish Church was subjected" (*WCF*, 20.1). The believer is also reminded that "God alone is Lord of the conscience" and has left it "free from the doctrines and commandments of men" (*WCF*, 20.2).

Watching children play games is always interesting. And when I say games, I mean outside games. I don't mean staring at the Nintendo Switch, but actually playing outdoors. Children and their games are funny because there's always that one child that changes the rules midway through the game—and always in his favor. You know the kid I am talking about. The ball has to touch this line or you have to stand still for this many minutes. The rules get changed mid-game, and he's mad if people won't play according to his rules.

That kid is in the church too—except he's a pastor or a church board or a whole denomination. The *Confession of Faith* is protecting the church from schoolyard-tantrum leadership that requires other Christians to play by their made-up rules. Christian liberty is freedom from guilt, freedom from the ordinances of the Old Testament, and freedom from the doctrines and traditions of men. The pastors and elders at Westminster had been in a context of a church that imposed rules that were not found in the Bible—and wisely, these pastors and teachers said, "We have had enough. Let the Bible be our rule book for faith and life; we are finished playing by your rules."

Are we free to keep the law of God? Yes. Are we free from the law's condemnation? Yes. Are we free from Old Testament ritual? Yes. Are we free from the teachings and traditions of men? Yes!

That's Christian liberty!

Worship and Rest

The *Confession* goes on to help us practice the Christian life in our worship and in our rest on the Lord's Day. Worship and rest—Sabbath—are two very important practices in the *Confession of Faith*. Worship is important because it is the primary way we give thanks to God for salvation in Jesus Christ.

Two points of interest stand out in the section on worship. The first is that God decides what worship should look like. This may be one of the most profound statements that the *Westminster Confession* makes. It says, "The acceptable way of worshiping the true God is instituted by himself" (*WCF*, 21.1). It goes on to say that God cannot be worshiped according to the "imaginations" of men, the "suggestions of Satan," or any other visible representation not prescribed in the Bible.

This book began by seeking to show the value of a confessional church. Having biblical worship that is familiar to your experience is one of the great values of confessionalism in the Christian life. The 1979 *Muppet Movie* has a scene where Fozzy Bear and Kermit the Frog pull their Studebaker into a church parking lot along an old country road. As they enter the building, there's a rock band—Dr. Teeth and the Electric Mayhem—playing at the front of the sanctuary. Fozzy turns to Kermit and says, "They don't look like Presbyterians to me!"

And that's true!

Presbyterians who take the *Confession of Faith* seriously worship God according to his Word!

The second point of interest in the worship section is how long it talks about prayer. Prayer is the theme of two whole paragraphs and mentioned in others. Other things we do in worship—sing, hear the Word read and preached, etc.—are only mentioned briefly. Prayer is central to Christian worship in the mind of the Westminster Assembly.

Worship and rest are to occupy the Lord's Day. The rhythm of life is six days of labor and one day of rest (Exod. 20:9–10). The rest component of the rhythm is called Sabbath in the *Confession of Faith*. Sabbath means rest.

Maybe you are asking questions such as:

Is Sabbath a moral principle or just a tradition?

How often should a Christian observe a Sabbath?

Why do Christians have Sabbath on Sunday where Jews have it on Saturday?

What does Sabbath preparation look like?

What do we rest from?

What do we do instead when we rest?

These questions, and more, are answered in chapter 21 of the *Confession of Faith*, and it is not a burdensome discussion—only eight paragraphs long.

Chapter 22 moves us from knowing the Christian life to living out Christian culture. Vows and oaths occur in our lives in various places. Church, weddings, the court room, and other places require vows and oaths, and according to the Westminster Assembly, vows and oaths are a big deal because they are in the presence of or toward God. Some Presbyterians—the Covenanters—were even called by that name because they took oaths and vows.

Maybe you've heard of them?

KNOWING CHRISTIAN CULTURE

The word culture brings different ideas to mind for different people. For some, culture means orchestras and tiny plates of French foods. For others, culture brings to mind pop music and skinny jeans. Culture, although a current buzz word in some circles, is a concept found in the *Westminster Confession* because unifying a Christian culture, or Christian community, was one of the stated goals of those at the Westminster Assembly. Three nations were to be united under one Christian culture and community.

The Christian life is not merely a "me and Jesus" life; it is lived in community—lived within a specific time and culture. Culture, which comes from the Latin word for "tend," has farming in mind.

The Christian individual is part of a society that tends, tills, and cares for that which God provides. Culture, not exhaustively discussed in the *Confession*, zeros in on two important cultural areas that brought confusion in the 17th century—government and marriage. Sounds like today, doesn't it?

And where should this type of discussion begin? The *Westminster Confession* begins here: "God, the supreme Lord and King of all the world" (*WCF*, 23.1). The starting point for culture—government and marriage—is God himself, the supreme Lord and King of all the world.

Government, we are told, is for our public good (*WCF*, 23.1), and this ordering of society occurs "with the power of the sword" for both encouragement and punishment, depending on whether a citizen does evil or good. Christians are permitted to pursue and work with government when called to do so (*WCF*, 23.2), and the first objective of the

Christian in government is to "especially . . . maintain piety." Government is to work with and support the church in seeing the kingdom of Jesus advanced. Christians who are in government, besides maintaining piety, ought to: 1) maintain justice, 2) maintain peace, 3) wage just wars.

Justice, peace, and war all sound like government work to our 21st-century ears, and yet the idea of maintaining piety is quite foreign to our understanding of the government's role. The Bible speaks a great deal about the role of the government in our lives and in relationship to God. Remember that God is the "supreme Lord and King of all the world;" therefore, he has plenty to say to the kings and lords of this world. Paragraph 3 of chapter 23 speaks further of those duties, although some have—with controversy—amended this section to sound . . . well . . . more American.

The chapter on government ends with a reminder that Christians have a duty toward those that lawfully govern over them:

Pray for them.

Honor them.

Pay taxes.

Obey lawful commands.

Be subject to their authority (for conscience' sake).

Living in a Christian culture would assume a Christian government. Although the *Confession* does not say everything that it could say about the government in chapter 23, there is a good framework for beginning to think about the role of government. But culture is more than the government and your relationship to it. The family is even more central to culture.

Pope John Paul II (not a Presbyterian) once said, "As the family goes, so goes the nation." He was right about that, for sure! Family plays an integral role in the well-being of a society. The *Confession* begins chapter 24 with the statement, "marriage is to be between one man and one woman." Following the "who" of marriage, the *Confession* moves on to the "why" as 24.2 is unfolded:

Marriage is for the "mutual help of husband and wife."

Marriage is for having children.

Marriage is for increasing "the church with an holy seed."

Marriage is for avoiding sexual sin.

Not all people think clearly when entering into marriage, so the reader is told to only marry "as such as profess the true reformed religion" (*WCF*, 24.3). Marriages that are unequally yoked are difficult and often lead to much marital conflict. Sometimes that conflict leads to marital difficulty and even divorce. How often have you heard people ask what the Bible says about divorce and what it means to seek a "lawful" divorce. The pastors and elders at Westminster envisioned that some unhappy people would seek to push the boundaries on divorce. Remember that the English

Reformation began with a divorce! "Nothing but adultery, or such willful desertion" (*WCF*, 24.6) are the reasons that the Bible gives for divorce.

Family life and one's relationship to the government make up the *Confession*'s statements on Christian culture. Does the *Confession* say everything that could be said about Christian culture? Of course not. Art and music and literature and economics and work ethic and a host of other things could have been talked about, but the two institutions that are often most important and most controversial needed to be discussed. The *Confession* then turns our attention to the church, an element of Christian culture that is of great importance. To the church, the *Westminster Confession* devotes six chapters.

KNOWING THE CHURCH

I collect things. One of the things that I have liked about collecting is the search. Whether it's for wheat-back pennies, a certain piece of pottery from the Ohio River Valley, or a first edition book, the search for an object is enjoyable. But when the object is found, the satisfaction is great.

This book began with a search. Where are the churches that teach the Bible? Where are the churches that demonstrate a connection to the history of God's people? Where are the churches that are honest enough to write down what they believe and teach and practice what they've written? The whole of the *Confession of Faith* has been seen as an interaction between the person of Jesus Christ and the church that he came to save. Chapters 25–31 of the *Westminster Confession* focus on what the church is to believe about itself.

Could you define the church?

Is church really necessary for Christians?

How do we look at churches that practice differently?

Is the Roman Catholic Church a true church?

What does communion of the saints mean?

When we talk about sacraments, is that biblical language?

How do we do the Lord's Supper?

What is baptism? Should we baptize babies?

What is church discipline?

Why do we have synods and councils?

What if I disagree with a decision of Synod?

Have you ever asked these or similar questions? The *Confession of Faith* answers all of them and more.

The "invisible church" is defined in 25.1 as the "whole number of the elect, that have been, are, or shall be gathered into one, under Christ." The visible church is made up of "all those throughout the world that profess the true religion; and of their children" and "out of which there is no ordinary possibility of salvation" (*WCF*, 25.2).

Important distinctions between visibility and invisibility, purity and impurity, and mixture and error are discussed before moving into chapter 26 that speaks "Of Communion of Saints." Fellowship with Christ and his church are essential aspects of the Christian life. How do we have communion with each other? Paragraph 2 helps us to understand that communion is:

Communion in the worship of God.

Communion in mutual fellowship.

Communion in meeting each other's needs.

The Psalms speak of the gathering of the people of God as a gathering of joy. Psalm 122 says, "'Now to the LORD's house let us go!' These words made me rejoice" (*The Book of Psalms for Worship*, 122B). The psalmist rejoices at the thought of being gathered with the people of God, and yet for so many believers, the church and her gatherings do not bring joy. Reviving the Bible's ideas of what the church is, as described in the *Westminster Confession of Faith*, can revitalize and revive Christians and churches as they rediscover the richness of the *Westminster Confession*.

Two important components of worship are given further attention in chapters 27, 28, and 29. First, the sacraments, which are "holy signs and seals of the covenant of grace," are discussed at length. Important questions around who is to be baptized and why bread and wine are the two elements of the Lord's Supper are answered. The Westminster Assembly wanted to help the church take hold of the grace the sacraments offer. This, after all, is their purpose.

A church committed to communion in worship, fellowship, and meeting the needs of others is demonstrating God's will for the church. Under the blessing of God, churches that are reflecting his will through this godly conformity will flourish in theological depth, numbers, and in love.

But the church does not always think and act as God would have her to. We are sinful people, and the Scriptures tell us that God disciplines those he loves (Heb. 12:6). The *Confession* spends chapter 30 explaining this need for Christian discipline: "Church censures," says the *Confession*,

> are necessary, for the reclaiming and gaining of offending brethren, for deterring of others from the like offenses, for pursuing out of that leaven which might infect the whole lump, for vindicating the honor of Christ, and the holy profession of the gospel, and for preventing the wrath of God, which might justly fall upon the church. (*WCF*, 30.3)

Elders and pastors are then shown the process of discipline and how to maintain it in the church.

Separating the back yard of my childhood home from a back neighbor was a flower garden. The older neighbor was not fond of kids walking through her yard, and during one trek through her grass, she caught me. As a young child, I was terrified of her. She called my father and told him that I was in her yard and then added a complete lie to the story: she claimed that I called her a name (a name I had never heard).

My dad spanked me for calling her the name, not for walking in her grass. I was spanked unjustly.

There are times in the church when matters of justice need to be determined. Chapter 31 unfolds the various reasons that God, in his providence, gave rule by elders and courts of appeals as the way in which the church is to be ordered:

To determine controversies of faith.

To determine cases of conscience.

To set down rules for better ordering public worship.

To set down rules for better governing the church.

To receive complaints of maladministration.

These court decisions are to be received "with reverence and submission" (*WCF*, 31.3) as long as they are consistent with the Word of God and yet, like the spanking received for a word I did not say, "all synods or councils . . . may err; and many have erred" (*WCF*, 31.4). The church is not perfect, yet we look to the One who is for our help and aid.

The Westminster Assembly was not idealistic about the church—they understood that there was an ideal that they aimed for and a reality in which they lived. A bird's-eye view of the Westminster Assembly's understanding of the church teaches the Christian to seek a pure church and to work within the context of a church that will have blind spots and error. It will not always be so. Let me write it again: it will not always be so.

The Christian will die and enter into glory looking at Jesus Christ face-to-face. The experience of "church" will be different then and, with that hope in mind, the assembly instructs us in how to die well—confident of the glory set before them.

KNOWING HOW TO DIE WELL

Death and taxes are inevitable, we are told. Preparation for taxes occurs at every paycheck and by April 15 of every year. We are ready for taxes. But how many fail to prepare for death? How many fail to get right with God before they return to dust in their bodies and have our souls "immediately return to God who gave them" (*WCF*, 32.1)?

Do we know how to die well? Preparation and knowledge of that which is to come help us. The Westminster Assembly ends the *Confession of Faith* with chapters 32–33: "Of the State of Men after Death, and of the Resurrection of the Dead," and "Of the Last Judgment."

In six paragraphs, the *Westminster Confession* concludes with showing the church that hope to which they look. The warning for those who refuse to rest in Christ's forgiveness is also held forth.

Christians "are received into the highest heavens, where they behold the face of God, in light and glory, waiting for the full redemption of their bodies" (*WCF*, 32.1). In contrast, the "souls of the wicked are cast into hell."

The hope of resurrection is discussed in the second and third paragraphs. The world shall then stand before Jesus "to whom all power and judgment is given of the Father" (*WCF*, 33.1).

The pastoral heart of the *Westminster Confession of Faith* and of the pastors and elders who wrote it comes out in the closing words:

> As Christ would have us to be certainly persuaded that there shall be a day of judgment, both to deter all men from sin; and for the greater consolation of the godly in their adversity: so will He have that day unknown to men, that they may shake off all carnal security, and be always watchful, because they know not at what hour the Lord will come; and may be ever prepared to say, Come, Lord Jesus, come quickly, Amen. (*WCF*, 33.3)

The closing words are so important because of the pastoral weight they carry. The Christian is asked to "shake off carnal security" and to "be always watchful" and to always say, "Come Lord Jesus, come quickly!"

The *Westminster Confession of Faith* has a framework for living biblically in one's heart, home, church, and culture. As we live, shaking off our own securities while being watchful, the Christian who embraces this *Confession* as his or her own is in a unique position to think biblically and systematically about the world in which we live. So much of Christianity is fluid today—and many do not want to wrestle through the eternal truths and orderly church life that grants stability in one's faith.

As you engage in a fuller study of the *Westminster Confession of Faith*, my hope is that you will remember the driving factors of its writing—a war, a heart for unity in the church, and a desire to conform teaching, worship, and piety to Scriptures. The hope is that you would either be renewed in your commitment to a confessional church or continue your journey to find one. We live in unstable times, and ancient foundations need to be restored. The Westminster Standards, building on ancient Christian truths, are relevant in the 21st century and provide much needed stability.

This stability—ancient and modern—allows me to say, "I have a confession."

Now you see why.

Come Lord Jesus, come quickly. Amen.

BOOKS MENTIONED

Barrett, Matthew. *God's Word Alone—The Authority of Scripture.* Zondervan Academic, 2016.

Beeke, Joel, and Paul M. Smalley. *Reformed Systematic Theology, Volume 1.* Crossway, 2019.

Dixhoorn, Chad B. Van. *Confessing the Faith.* Banner of Truth, 2014.

Education Digest, The, Volume 58. 1992.

Foxe, John. *Foxe's Book of Martyrs.* Jazzybee Verlag, 2012.

Helopolous, Jason. "The Examined Life." *Tabletalk.* October 2017.

Henry, Matthew. *Matthew Henry's Commentary on the Whole Bible.* Hendrickson Pub, 2019.

Knox, John. *The Works of John Knox: 6 Volume Set.* Banner of Truth, 2014.

Letham, Robert. *The Westminster Assembly*.

Lewis, C. S. *Miracles*. Harper Collins, 2009.

Manton, Thomas. *The Works of Thomas Manton*. Sovereign Grace Publishers, 2002.

Miller, Samuel. *Doctrinal Integrity*. 1989.

Shelley, Bruce Leon. *Church History in Plain Language*. Thomas Nelson Incorporated, 1995.

The Book of Psalms for Worship. Crown & Covenant Publications, 2011.

The Westminster Confession of Faith.

Turrettin, Francis. *Institutes of Elenctic Theology*. Presbyterian & Reformed Publishing Company, 1997.

Westminster Larger Catechism. Good Press.

GRASSMARKET PRESS

GRASSMARKET PRESS is named for the square in Edinburgh where many Reformed Presbyterians (also known as Covenanters) were martyred for preaching Jesus Christ's reign over Scotland and all earth. Though many lost their lives, their witness for Christ endures. Grassmarket Press aims to help Christians know, practice, and stand for their faith.

THE BEDROCK SERIES aims to provide clear, concise books on Christian doctrine and life from a Reformed and Presbyterian perspective.